2.50 ✓

WITHDRAWN
From Toronto Public Library

Wednesday Morning

Wednesday Morning

by

Robert John Renison

McCLELLAND AND STEWART, LIMITED
Publishers
TORONTO   CANADA

COPYRIGHT CANADA 1944
BY
THE SUTHERLAND PRESS, LIMITED
ST. THOMAS

DEDICATED
TO
MY WIFE

Preface

THE TITLE OF THIS BOOK is an acknowledgment to Mr. C. George McCullagh of the *Globe and Mail* who has encouraged me to publish a selection of articles which have appeared in the paper weekly for more than seven years.

The contents give a picture of a typical year in contemporary Canadian life. Perhaps the name may suggest that Religion is not only relevant on Sunday but especially for our working days. I hope that those who read may find the morning view of a prospector.

ROBERT JOHN RENISON.

June, 1944.

Contents

CHAPTER		PAGE
1.	One Day at a Time	3
2.	The Way of a Wandering Star	6
3.	The Springs of Life	10
4.	The Lake of the Dead	13
5.	The Rivers of Damascus	16
6.	The Church that Would Not Die	19
7.	The Message of the Pyramids	22
8.	The Nightingale of the Psalms	25
9.	The Consistency of the Bible	29
10.	The Hunger of the Soul	32
11.	The Christian Quadrilateral	35
12.	The People and the Church	38
13.	Is Anyone There?	41
14.	The Hopefulness of God	44
15.	The Ethics of Pain	47
16.	I Hate Lent	50
17.	Battle in the Desert	53
18.	Stones and Bread	56
19.	Sensation and Religion	59
20.	The Empire of Christ	62
21.	The Second Watch	65
22.	Forgiveness	68
23.	The Little Hills	71
24.	Thoughts About Evil	75
25.	Calvary	78

CHAPTER		PAGE
26.	Tragedy and the Crucifixion	81
27.	"The Son of Man"	84
28.	The Voice of the Wounded	87
29.	The Voice of a Son	90
30.	'When It Was Dark'	93
31.	Recognition In Eternity	96
32.	"A-wearying for Christ"	99
33.	Under One Roof	102
34.	The Miracle of Spring	105
35.	Summer and Winter	108
36.	"The Glorious Company"	110
37.	The Plain Man and the Trinity	114
38.	The Brittannic-American Brotherhood	117
39.	An Empire's Bivouac	121
40.	The Soldier's Religion	124
41.	Greater Love Hath No Man	129
42.	The Well of Bethlehem	132
43.	The Women of England	135
44.	Coventry	138
45.	The Magnetism of Sacrifice	141
46.	The Miracles of Christ	144
47.	Christ's Gentleman	147
48.	The Conquest of Fear	151
49.	The Hills of Life	154
50.	In Praise of the Moon	157
51.	The Climate of Religion	160
52.	Portrait of St. Paul	163
53.	The World of Books	166
54.	Why We Pray	169
55.	The Missionary	172
56.	The Mystic Stairs	175
57.	Is Christianity Dying?	178

CHAPTER		PAGE
58.	'The Christian Headache'	181
59.	Religion Makes the Front Page	184
60.	Castles in Spain	187
61.	Sixty Years After	190
62.	A Divided Personality	193
63.	"The Candle of the Lord"	196
64.	The Blessedness of Work	199
65.	Music	202
66.	The Four Vitamins	205
67.	The Fourth Commandment	208
68.	The Second Half of Religion	211
69.	The Ivory Gates	214
70.	"I Go Afishing"	217
71.	The Wings of the Morning	221
72.	Canada Through a Telescope	225
73.	The Invisible City	228
74.	"Known to God"	230
75.	Advent	233
76.	The Last Enemy	236
77.	Indian Christmas	239
78.	"Then Jesus Came"	242
79.	Bethlehem, Goodnight	245
80.	"The Insubstantial Pageant"	248
81.	Sunset	251
82.	The Bivouac of Time	255
83.	Tramp or Pilgrim	258
84.	The Romance of the Explorer	261
85.	The Tragedy of the Explorer	265
86.	Man, the Enemy	269
87.	Invasion	272

Foreword

FOREWORDS, AS THOSE who read them have observed, are commonly written by men of achievement and distinction; seldom by the undistinguished and obscure; rarely by a man of business. I have written this at the request of the Bishop, whom one does not refuse.

Wednesday Morning is something more than a book of little sermons. In an amazingly spontaneous and unselfconscious way it is a revelation of the author, more candid than an autobiography. The chapters, so timely, so topical, which make up Wednesday Morning, came out week by week in the Wednesday morning edition of the *Globe and Mail* in order "that people might have a taste of religion between Sundays." They have appealed to all classes and have been cut out and pasted, as they appeared, in many a scrap book throughout the country. Most of them I have heard him preach. Reduced to writing, practiced and accomplished speaker though he is, "The Little Meditations," as he calls them, seem to have lost nothing, but rather to have gained, since one may read them at his own pace and turn back where he chooses to savor their quality and the Preacher's thought.

The impression the Bishop makes in preaching or writing is that of a man who has had time to think.

He is never hurried. He preaches and writes as simply and naturally as he talks, in the idiom of his day. How pungent and arresting are his words! "He found a lunatic among the tombs and made him into a missionary." He takes someone of whom we have thought as a stiff-necked stained glass saint and transforms him into a real man who has something on the ball. No mean poet, he is a master of English prose. He has an unerring instinct "for the shape and ring of sentences," pithy, trenchant and profound. The meditations are packed with them.

Like Conrad, he can "Cause the light of magic suggestiveness to play for an evanescent instant over the commonplace surface of words, of the old, old words, worn thin, defaced by ages of careless usage." He achieves the aim of the preacher and the writer, to make us feel, to make us see. His style, simple and direct, is the result of ceaseless and unremitting study of the World's Great Books, the Bible, Shakespeare, Pilgrim's Progress and the Greek and Roman Classics. "By what long discipline," says Thoreau, "and at what cost a man learns to speak simply at last."

The first chapter, "One Day at a Time," points the way in which they should be read and re-read, for they will bear re-reading "One Day at a Time!"

There is something of the genius of O. Henry in his choice of titles and his treatment of his themes. "Battle in the Desert," "The Four Vitamins," "The Blessedness of Work," "The Christian Headache," "The Nightingale of the Psalms," "The Hopefulness of God," "Invasion." The haunting titles and what he says under them take hold of one and linger in the memory like things learned in childhood.

xiv

He has a fresh and startling way of saying things. To illustrate the sustained excellence of his style one may pick passages anywhere in the book. The temptation to quote in extenso is almost irresistible.

"Trinity Sunday is not a War Dance over heretics."

"Our Redeemer was not an angel flying over the tree-tops of life, but a man walking on a stony road. Millions who would lose sight of the angel will gladly follow the man."

"We can now see with clearer eyes than ever before the beauty and meaning of kindly faces and the magic of the common tasks of plain people who go to their work in the morning and return to their wives and children as the sun goes down."

"It is only by moving, only by following the star, that man accomplishes a journey which brings him within sight of the city of God."

Of the old Indian in "Sixty Years After"—"He was the last of the Mohicans, and as he prayed to Kitchemuneto he spoke of the life of man as a tale that is told by the campfire, and asked that he might rejoin those that he had known and loved in the eternal camping ground."

Of a theory of our cosmos, "The universe was originally unconscious, but became creative as it went along, developing some real novelties in its progress."

Of St. Paul, "He does not seem to understand women, which is probably why he is not their favorite Saint." Of Matthew, "He was a business man, and a shady business at that." Of another, "Like a sick eagle on the branch of a tree, regarding the world with a lack-lustre eye."

Widely travelled and deeply read, Bishop Renison brings home to us again that the value of travel depends on the knowledge that one carries with him. The

Odyssey of his journeyings is a fascinating record. He is a part of all that he has met. "He makes us pause, to glance for a moment at the surrounding vision of form and color." What an eye he has for the beautiful, what a sense of the dramatic! He takes us with him to the shores of Hudson's Bay to an Indian Christmas Service in the little Church of Moosonee where we can smell the new-cut spruces. We see the wild geese flying north and flying south. We follow him on snowshoes among "the rocks and Christmas trees of Northern Ontario." He takes us over the Great Northern Lakes and down the majestic Mackenzie to that Arctic Sea that lies, "yellow as a snake's belly" athwart its mouth. He transports us in a bomber to England, to Coventry. We journey with him into that wine-dark Sea that washes the shores of ancient Mediterranean civilizations—Egypt, Carthage, Rome, Greece and the Isles of Greece; to the Hellespont, the walls of Troy, Phoenicia, Syria and the Holy Land, where we see the snow-capped mountains of the Near East and feel the power of the Syrian sun as we descend the long dusty road to Jericho in the canyon of the Jordan, to the heavy salt waters of the "Sodomite Sea"; to Mount Quarantania, "where we might have seen the weary meditative figure of Christ, with nothing visible to the human eye except the circling eagle in the sky and the flitting of some desert animal passing beneath the hill;" to Nazareth, "That eagle's nest in the Galilean Hills," to Bethlehem, to Jerusalem, where he speaks of Pilate and Caiaphas, and at last to "The ignoble hillock of Golgotha, littered with dead men's skulls, changed by Jesus into Calvary where the mystic Cross towers over the wrecks of time."

"Of the making of many books," saith the Preacher,

"there is no end," but here is a book of infinite variety, straight from a mind, "rich with the spoils of time." Here is wisdom, mysticism, breadth of sympathy, tolerance and understanding. Here is religion, travel, history, philosophy, poetry and the drama of life, and pictures, pictures, always pictures, drawn with the deft, bold strokes of a master craftsman with the seeing eye, the passing parade of mankind through the ages.

ROBERT LYNCH STAILING.

Toronto, May 12th, 1944.

Wednesday Morning

1

One Day at a Time

As we enter the mystic gates of a new era we are reminded of the countless ages since this planet was swirling star dust and the lesser period during which the endless procession of human feet have walked the path of the years toward the setting sun. For a few fleeting moments we are thrilled and humbled by the thought that life is a pilgrimage and that every one of us is a traveller.

In the ancient book of Deuteronomy there are a couple of sentences of the farewell song of Moses, which the dying hero left to his people. They are words for all ages, especially for our own nervous generation at the beginning of a year which many are facing with fear.

"As thy days, so shall thy strength be. . . .
The eternal God is thy refuge, and underneath are
the everlasting arms."

Here is a promise which is medicine for people who have come to believe that common folk are merely pawns on a chess board of pitiless sky. Not as your life is, not as your years are, but as your days so shall your strength be. One day at a time is all we have. The way to live in any period of history, but especially in years like these, is just a day at a time. The number of deaths and nervous breakdowns due to neglect of this Divine warning is beyond computation.

3

Jesus Christ lived a day at a time and He told His disciples to do the same, "Sufficient unto the day is the evil thereof."

In simpler ages this was the method of life for the world's pioneers. Before the coming of radio, telegraph and airplanes the world was safer than it is at present. Half the horrors of the world are the anticipation of what never comes. If God had meant us to bear the burdens of next month He would have given us the power to see that far.

It is somewhat amusing to find that city people take it for granted that the men of the North need nothing but strong backs and tireless arms. The pioneer in Northern Ontario is not only an athlete, but a man who understands the secret of triumphant life. Long before there were airplanes he travelled in his frail canoe, a master of the rapids, but perfectly willing to portage when he must.

The paddle and the axe preach a sermon on the text, "As thy days, so shall thy strength be."

All through the nineteenth century men regularly went to the Arctic Ocean from Peace River Crossing and back. All the power was from slender pine blades in sinewy hands—one hundred and twenty strokes a minute, fourteen hours a day for four months; no worry beyond the next camping place in the evening. If Alexander Mackenzie had stopped to count the millions of splashes his paddles would make, he never would have won immortality.

A man, an axe and a clump of pines standing in the snow. The odds seem hopeless, for those trunks are like tall masts. But one swing at a time, with rhythmic ease, the axe falls and at nightfall there is a pile of fuel to heat a house for weeks and a man only pleasantly tired sits down to supper, "As thy days, so shall thy strength be."

4

The second line gives the source of human power. "The eternal God is thy refuge." The words suggest that God has been with our fathers; that history is luminous with His presence. It is a wonderful comfort to feel that there is a retreat to which we can fly from the storms of life. For God is the true home of the soul. There is something within us that calls to Him when life becomes too exacting. In Him we may renew our strength for each succeeding day. We should probably be much happier and more serene if we made it our daily habit to seek rest where it can be found.

"Underneath are the Everlasting Arms." Here we have the suggestion of the personality of God—not "Underneath are the everlasting laws"—but warm and tender, faithful and strong, the arms of the Divine love. Notice that the arms are underneath us, not always holding us, but ready to catch us when we fall.

We are living in an age of anxiety and doubt. Sir Edward Grey said in 1914: "The lights are going out all over Europe and they will not be lighted again in our lifetime." For many the future is dark because the old charts have been thrown overboard and the sanctions of our childhood are challenged. Here we are on the shore of unknown islands. What message has God for us?

To weary business men with great responsibilities; to a multitude of anxious fathers who are near the breaking point because they have had no opportunity to provide for the families; to mothers who cannot sleep because they wonder what their growing children will do or what they may be called upon to bear; to those who dread this new year, God says, "Live one day at a time." "As thy days, so shall thy strength be. . . . The Eternal God is thy refuge, for underneath are the everlasting arms."

5

2

The Way of a Wandering Star

THERE IS NO STORY in all the world more beautiful than this. There is the wistfulness of long wandering about these strangers, star-guided across the desert. We know little of the Magi. Tradition says there were three of them, and the story of Ben Hur has given the legend to the world. But the Bible simply calls them the Wise Men from the East. They were students who were also seekers. They were men on the alert, searching the skies and the records. They were investigators, the scientific men of their age, pondering the old, watching for the new. Men say that the thinkers have deserted the Church. It has never been completely true. It is not true today. Pascal and Pasteur, Kelvin and Oliver Lodge were all Christians. But the Church has often failed to welcome the Wise Men, and has doubted their gifts. It was harder for the Wise Men to come than for the shepherds. They had a less obvious sign to descry, a longer journey to take, but they brought more. It is still the same. It is harder for the thinker to find Christ, but when he comes he has more to bring.

We notice in the first place that these were men of vision. They had the sense of poetry. They were alive to the suggestiveness of common things. There was a touch of inspiration about them. Let it be frankly admitted that

6

their wisdom did more for them and led them to a richer and more generous emotion than many a man's scientific knowledge today. They were ready for any clue wherever it might lead them. Routine scientists abound, but radium, the X-ray, and chloroform would never have been discovered if wise men had not followed a star. Again, we notice that the star led to something higher and brighter still. It aroused them to activity. We can believe more easily in something that leads men to action than in something that throws them into slumber. The star stirred a pulse in these men that would not let them rest. To them it was something more than a beautiful spectacle, it was more than an ordinary star. It was His star. The moment you attribute personality to any object its value is changed. It may be worth little itself, but because of its personal associations it is worth its weight in gold.

Once more, these men were not merely travellers, but reverent travellers. "We have seen His star and are come to worship Him." They had the gift of wonder. These men saw and fell down and gave. They did not give without seeing, as so much modern charity does. Many are willing to be generous who are too proud to bow their spirit in worship, but liberality will not be accepted by God in lieu of worship. Where there is no wonder there is no romance. The golden mystery has faded from the landscape, the flowers are botanical specimens, the stars are cold, glittering points of light. When you have shut the star out of your heart you have no city of dreams.

No man who values his sanity and the progress of the race can afford to sneer at the poetry of Nature if it keeps alive such visions as these. There is nothing sentimental in the idea that Nature is talking to us, that other worlds are interested in ours, that the stars are trying to call us to

God. Each man brought gifts from his own land. The gold was from India, the frankincense from Persia, the myrrh from Arabia. Each man brought what he had. And so the gift will never be that which grows in another's country. It will not be some better or nobler thing than what you have, but just that. "Your own redeemed personality" is the one gift which God values most. For the grown man gold stands for the secular life of work and politics. It includes business capacity, genius in art, literature or science. All this region is the royal domain of man's secular interest and power.

Perhaps God will some day make you a Wise Man by taking you on a strange journey through the Slough of Despond and the River of Sorrow. There are some who know it well. They are acquainted with grief, with loneliness, with anxiety and bereavement. They have sorrowed much and felt pain and death around them in the world. Their hearts are full of a great compassion. It is the myrrh that grows in their country, and that will be the perfect offering.

It was night time. It must have been, for the star was shining in the sky overhead. What difference could that Child make to the world that was and the world that was to be?

> That night when in Judaean skies
>   The mystic star dispensed its light,
> A blind man turned him in his sleep
>   And dreamed that he had sight.
>
> That night when in a stable stall
>   Slept Child and Mother in humble fold,
> A cripple turned his twisted form
>   And dreamed that he was whole.

8

That night when to the Mother's breast
  A little King was held secure,
A harlot slept a happy sleep
  And dreamed that she was pure.

That night when in the manger lay
  The Holy One Who came to save,
A man turned in the sleep of death
  And dreamed there was no grave.

3

The Springs of Life

MANY OF THE WORD PICTURES of the Bible have little reality
to the mind of the average Canadian, and this is true in
the emphasis on the life-giving quality of water. Ours is
a land of lakes and rivers, though the tragedy of the
drought area on the prairies may remind us that even
this northern land is not immune from thirst. It cannot
be said that there is no hunger, but, generally speaking, a
cup of cold water can be found anywhere from the
Atlantic to the Pacific Ocean.

But in the old storied lands of the Bible, even the fertile
areas are surrounded by waterless deserts—a country
where the rivers are swallowed up in the sands so that
they never reach the sea. When the modern traveller
drives in a motor car from Beirut to Damascus, as soon as
he passes the ridge of Lebanon he looks down on an
ocean of yellow sand. It would seem that no city could
exist fifty miles to the east, but, after a few miles, the
crystal clear waters from the top of Mount Hermon are
seen running on both sides of the road, and in a little
while you are shaded by orchards of palms, peaches and
pepper trees, as the Abana widens out into many laughing
streams from the mountain-tops, giving life and hope to
men and women and also to a thirsty land.

The word "thirst" in such climates suggests the idea of the most passionate and painful craving that a man may endure. If not quenched, it leads to certain death. Many of the most beautiful passages in the Bible speak of the thirst of the soul. "As the hart panteth after the water brooks, so panteth my soul after Thee, O God." The sweet Psalmist of Israel who tended his flock on the rim of the desert could write, "He leadeth me beside the still waters"—a perfect picture of the rapture of the spirit of man.

Before we leave the shores of our human existence by the Sea of Eternity, whence we come, in the earlier years the spirit of youth passes through the pleasant foothills of buoyant experience, but, sooner or later, we reach the long, dreary road to middle life, where there are little time and little opportunity to find spiritual refreshment.

For a long journey a vessel is not enough, because, although a vessel holds water, our souls need a spring that comes from the fir-clad hills of God. The most modern reservoir may run dry. It needs constant replenishing from without. The spring has the supply within itself. There is a picture of human life. The happy are they who have inward resources, who find their happiness from the well within; and that is what Christ offers us in the region of the spirit. The soul in touch with Him has access to a Fount of Living Water.

It would be possible to speak at length of the streams which come from the Eternal Springs—faith, hope, joy and love—but it is not necessary. There are others. The result of the habit of worship or the lack of it may not show in a few days or even in a few years. It is like the growth and the destruction of the verdure on the hills. All the water in the streams and the fresh springs in the valleys of life are from the reservoir of the forest soil into which the rains of God are gathered. "I will lift up mine eyes unto the hills from whence cometh my help."

The mountain-tops are not only a beautiful picture to the eye; they are a promise of water to the thirsty soul. Even in the middle of August the yellow slopes of Hermon are mottled with great patches of snow which look insignificant but which fill the canyons one hundred feet deep in the hottest time of the year.

So it is with life. There are many of us who wonder why existence appears so arid and dusty and dead—for there are many people who have everything to live for and nothing to live by. The reason is that we have let the Spiritual Springs go dry. In this busy, disenchanted world we are wise when we keep the channels open that lead to the Springs of the Love of God.

4

The Lake of the Dead

PALESTINE is a wonderful land for pictures. The high hills are like observation posts, for there are few trees and the clear air is like a telescope.

As you stand on the outskirts of Bethlehem there is a wonderful view eastward. A few hundred yards away on the slope lie the fields where the shepherds watched their flocks by night, and twenty miles away the eye catches the long, narrow line of the Jordan, like the handle of an antique spoon filled with melted sky. This spot of blue is the fabulous Dead Sea. It is a lake forty-seven miles long and ten miles wide, fourteen hundred feet below the level of the Mediterranean Sea.

When you motor down from Jerusalem by the Jericho Road you find that all the stories told by medieval travellers are false. In a ton of Atlantic water there are thirty pounds of salt; in the Dead Sea, in each ton, there are two hundred pounds of salt and other minerals. There is no animal life on the shores, for there is no food. There are no sea birds, for there are no fish. You will see no shells on the beach or plants of any kind. The waters are as dead as if they were on the moon. And yet, at sunset, it is beautiful as the dark hills are shadowed on its mirror. They say that under its waters lie the bones of Sodom and Gomorrah. What is the secret of this phenomenon of death in the midst of loveliness?

It is because this lake is a selfish sponge rotting in the sun. It has no outlet. It keeps every drop of the living waters of Jordan that flows into it right down from Hermon—for itself. It has no outlet for its life except evaporation.

Here is a modern parable from the land of parables. How are we to make our lives helpful? The Great Teacher who told the story of the Good Samaritan must have been thinking of the sight of the Dead Sea, which He often saw as He crossed the Jordan at Jericho, when He said, "Whosoever will save his life shall lose it."

Just sixty miles north of the Dead Sea there is another lake called Galilee. It is shaped like a heart. The same water flows into it as that which runs down to the Dead Sea—but it is laughing with life. There are oleanders at Tiberias and palms in the garden of the Franciscans in Capernaum. The eagles wheel down from the heights of Gadara and the water rushes out at one end of the lake as fast as it runs in at the other. The Lake of Galilee gets and it gives. It is a fountain, and that is what man's life ought to be.

Most of us take whatever we can get and do not care much how it comes as long as all goes well. We pride ourselves on the great democratic institutions that are our heritage, but very few citizens in Canada see to it that they give of their time and ability to make our country what it ought to be. Democracy in the nineteenth century was sure that it had conquered the world. It is the complacency and selfishness of the people who had the ball at their feet which has roused the debtor nations to madness.

14

But it is in the religious sphere that this truth can be best illustrated.

No one can fail to observe that Christianity is fighting for its life today. That does not mean that it is dying. It only means that the Church of Christ is asked by candid and sometimes hostile critics to justify itself.

Some people say, "Why missions?" forgetting that the original gospel was a wide-world adventure. Christianity needs new markets. As soon as the Church settles down to a condition of meditative self-admiration the hand-writing will be on the wall. A genuine revival of the missionary spirit would probably do more than any one thing to save civilization.

5

The Rivers of Damascus

ONE OF THE FIRST and greatest of the arts given to
humanity is the power to tell a story. With the world-
wide spread of education, for some reason or other the
simplicity of narration seems to become formal and life-
less. There is a glory in the roll of Homer's majestic lines
like the waves of his wine-colored seas. In the same way
the Old Testament gives us some of the most dramatic
pictures in literature.

We remember that unforgettable scene when Naaman
the Syrian, the hero of his country, at the instigation of a
little slave girl who waited on his wife, came in pomp
and circumstance to the door of the Prophet of Israel to
be cured of his leprosy. Elisha did not even give him an
interview, but told him to wash seven times in the River
Jordan and he would be healed. How human is the scorn
of Naaman as he cries: "Are not Abana and Pharpar,
rivers of Damascus, better than all the waters of Israel?
May I not wash in them and be clean?" There is something more than stupid patriotism in the words of the
stricken hero, because he came from a city whose rivers
were the delight of the ancient world.

Damascus lies on the edge of the desert less than two
hundred miles northeast of Jerusalem, the oldest city in

the world. It was a metropolis when Abraham was young. It has been conquered many times, but the victors have passed away and it remains. Today as the traveller drives in a modern car from the port of Beirut along seventy miles of perfect highway over the Lebanon range, climbing to four thousand feet in hairpin turns, in the distance to the right he may see Mount Hermon, nine thousand feet high, even in July covered with a reservoir or snow. It seems as if this modern road must lead to desolation as the caravans of camels are sighted shuffling through the soft sand toward the sea coast; but about twenty miles from Damascus suddenly little trickling streams of water are noticed coming down the hillside from Hermon, and in a short time they have merged into a clear, laughing river of ice-cold green water, the beginning of the ancient Abana, now called Barada. The Barada, with its tributary stream, the Pharpar, is the life of Damascus. Along many channels it runs through the city, and many of the homes and palaces are built over the waters. The city itself is like a diamond set in emeralds where the East meets the West. Far more than Rome it deserves the name, "The Eternal City."

On the other hand the Jordan, which flows south from Hermon, is an unattractive river. Owing to the country through which it flows, its waters are yellow and bitter, and it rushes down into the strangest canyon in the whole world, through the Lake of Galilee into the Dead Sea, fifteen hundred feet below the Mediterranean. As Naaman waded his horses across the Jordan he must have contrasted it with the crystal waters of his own city.

There is a parallel in these two rivers. The Abana is a symbol of all the delightful things that culture, education and commerce can supply. The Jordan is a picture of the people who made it famous—it is the river of religion.

Matthew Henry, the old commentator, has said: "He might wash in the rivers of Damascus and be clean from dirt, but he could not wash in them and be clean from leprosy."

In the old days leprosy was a type of sin. The mystery of its origin and the impossibility of its cure made that comparison to simple people an inevitable thing.

We have in our modern world many excellent rivers, but the waters of Israel are still the world's hope—a sinful soul may still wash in the Jordan and be clean.

6

The Church that Would Not Die

ON THE BANKS of the Bosphorus on one of the most beautiful sites in the world, in the ancient city of Constantinople, still stands the church of the eternal wisdom, St. Sophia. On the same spot there were two earlier churches. The last, in which John Chrysostom's golden voice was heard, was destroyed by fire in the year 404.

The present building was erected by the Emperor Justinian the Great, who restored for a time the glories of ancient Rome. Since the year 558 it has stood through the ages, for 900 years unchallenged the Queen of all Christian fanes, and for nearly 500 years the most famous Mohammedan mosque in the world. It is built in the shape of a Greek cross, about 250 feet square and nearly 200 feet high. The great pillars are of marble and stone. There are no fewer than 109 columns. They were taken from the temple of the ancient world, and every color of marble known to antiquity is to be seen in the great colonnade. Justinian gathered the treasures of all the ancient world for this cathedral, and on the day of its consecration is said to have exclaimed, "O Solomon, I have vanquished thee."

In the year 1204 the Fourth Crusade was diverted from

its objective, and the Crusaders committed one of the greatest religious crimes in history in conquering and sacking Constantinople. The treasures of St. Sophia were scattered all over the world. The picture of the Virgin, reputed to have been painted by St. Luke, is in the Cathedral at Genoa, and the bronze horses over the entrance of St. Mark at Venice were stolen by the Crusaders. (In 1797 the latter were purloined by Napoleon to adorn the Arc de Triomphe, where they remained for seventeen years before being returned to Venice). The Eastern Empire never recovered from this betrayal, and in the middle of the fifteenth century Mohammed II rode his horse through the open door into the sanctuary and stopped the last Mass that was celebrated in St. Sophia.

Many of the greatest modern churches have been inspired by its architecture. St. Peter's in Rome, St. Paul's in London, St. Mark's in Venice are in a sense its daughters, while every great Mohammedan mosque is almost a literal copy.

The Moslem conquerors destroyed many of the Christian symbols and methodically covered the glorious mosaics of the interior with plaster. In the last ten years the new Turkish government has turned this church into a museum. The prayer rugs are taken from the floor, and experts are now removing the plaster from the walls. At the great entrance over the door there is a mosaic just uncovered which has not been seen by human eyes for 500 years. In the centre the Virgin is seated with the Infant Christ in her arms. On the right stands Constantine, who presents a model of the city of Constantinople, and on the left Justinian with a miniature of St. Sophia in his hands.

In the central dome there is a faint outline of Christ with His hands outstretched in blessing after all the centuries of glory and darkness. May it not be a symbol of the Christ of our modern world?

7

The Message of the Pyramids

ON THE VERY EDGE of the desert, overlooking the Nile, stand the three great Pyramids which were built about five thousand years ago. The largest of the three—the Pyramid of Gizeh— is built of solid blocks of stone. Its base covers thirteen acres of ground and is one hundred and fifty feet higher than St. Paul's Cathedral. Its area is almost three times greater than that of St. Peter's in Rome.

When one considers that the stones of the Pyramids were dragged for many miles by hand from the mountains across the Nile and that they had to be rolled up to their position by one hundred thousand slaves who toiled for thirty years, one wonders for the reason of it all.

At one time the whole surface of the Pyramids was covered with marble, but for several hundred years it was used as a quarry to build the mosques and palaces of Cairo, in the days when the Moslem Sultans took no interest in archeology.

Just beyond the Pyramid the Sphinx lies on her bed of stone. The figure is too well known to describe, but it may be said that it is one hundred and twenty feet long and sixty feet in height at the head. It has the body of a lion, the head of a man and the face of a woman. The cheeks still show the enduring quality of the rouge, if not

22

of the lipstick, which was popular five millenniums ago. For many centuries all excepting the head was covered, but it is now excavated down to the base. It is a living thing. The swish of the tail is ominous. The abnormally gigantic claws seem to be dug into the bedrock for a spring, and the poor, mutilated face, still full of character, which was a target for the gunners of Napoleon, yet looks out over the desert. The Sphinx seems to be asking the meaning of human life.

Above the Nile, Osiris asks
Under a sapphire sky
"Have ye excelled old Pharaoh's tasks?"
The Sphinx leers, "Tell me why?"

These strange figures which were built before Abraham set out on his long journey from Haran to the Promised Land still stand almost perfect in that dry, Eastern clime, and they will probably continue to remain there when every modern work of man is nothing but ruins.

The thought of immortality is as old as humanity. Man has always believed that this life was not the end. It is true when we go back through the centuries to the very beginning of human history and it is certainly strange that in ancient Mexico there are to be found pyramids with the same message and the same general idea. It would seem that there must have been some historical connection, long before the days of Atlantis, between the Eastern and the Western continents of this planet.

James Anthony Froude, in one of his beautiful essays, points out that the Egyptians lived to die. Life with them was only a preparation for their death and burial. This is only one side of religion, and he goes on to remind us

23

that when the Children of Israel crossed the Dead Sea it was the beginning of a new era in religious history. Certainly at its earliest stages the religion of the Old Testament laid emphasis on man's responsibilities in this life and, with prophetic insight, the great historian forty years ago prophesied that Christianity itself in the next generation would perhaps turn to the adaptation of religion to the social problems of our own generation.

Any one who studies the spirit of Christianity in our present age will see how these two elements are fighting for supremacy in every Church in Christendom today.

There is one element in the Christian Church which says that the world can hardly be redeemed and that the Church should spend its time and exercise its commission to remind men of a life where there is no more toil, no more sin and no more death.

There are other prophets who are continually reminding us that it is the duty of Christians to make this world a better place to live in, and that a Church that has claimed the loyalty and love of man for nearly two thousand years should remember that its Founder was interested in the problems and sufferings of those whom He came to save.

8

The Nightingale of the Psalms

HENRY WARD BEECHER has written a tribute to the most famous religious poem in the Bible. It is a privilege to bring it to our world, which needs a song: "The 23rd Psalm is the nightingale of the Psalms. It is small, of a homely feather, singing shyly out of obscurity, but, oh, it has filled the air of the whole world with melodious joy. Blessed be the day on which that Psalm was born! What would you say of a pilgrim commissioned by God to travel up and down the earth singing a strange melody which when once heard causes every one to forget whatever sorrow he had? And so this singing angel goes on his way through all lands, singing in the language of every nation, driving away trouble by the pulses of the air which his tongue moves with Divine power. This song has charmed more griefs to rest than all the philosophy of the world. It has chained in their dungeon more evil thoughts, more black doubts, more thieving sorrows, than there are sands on the seashore. It has comforted the noble host of the poor; it has sung courage to the army of the disappointed; it has poured balm and consolation into the hearts of the sick, of captives in dungeons, of widows in their pinching griefs, of orphans in their loneliness. Dying soldiers have died easier as it

25

was read to them. Ghastly hospitals have been illuminated. It has visited the prisoner and broken his chains, and, like Peter's angel, led him forth in imagination and sung him back to his home again. It has made the dying Christian, the slave, freer than his master, and consoled those whom, dying, he left behind. And its work is not yet done. It will go on singing to our children through all generations of time, nor will it fold its wings until the last pilgrim is safe and time ended. And then it shall fly back to the bosom of God whence it came, and sing on, mingled with all those sounds of celestial joy which make Heaven musical for ever."

The Hebrew people were a race of shepherds. Living on the border of the desert, the mystery and the poetry of the shepherd's life was woven into their very soul. Far away on the lone mountain, with the everlasting hills around and heaven above, pure, blue, and high, and still, the solitary life threw men back upon themselves. And when that shepherd lad on the hills of Bethlehem first thought of God as the Shepherd of Souls it was one of the great moments in the history of mankind. Psalmist and prophet alike went to the shepherd and the flock to illustrate the care of God for His people. But in the Old Testament the shepherd is always more than a figure or an illustration—he is a historical fact.

No image used by Our Lord to illustrate His work has so touched the imagination of man as that of the Good Shepherd. For at least two centuries before any known attempt at a portrait of Christ, the popular devotion of the early Christians had covered the walls of the Catacombs with the figure of the Shepherd. Sometimes He stands with a lamb on His shoulders. Sometimes the sheep surround Him, looking up to be fed at His hands.

26

Sometimes He is seated and gathers His flock around Him to the strain of the shepherd's pipe. The symbol of the Good Shepherd sufficed all that the early Church needed in the way of a picture of her Lord.

There are three allegories in the 10th chapter of St. John. They are allegories rather than parables. The difference is that an allegory is a stained-glass window— you can see through it. A parable is a painting on canvas—it has substance of its own. The first scene is in the morning, the dew on the ground, the shepherds coming to claim their sheep. Sometimes a robber climbs the wall. The fold is simply a high stone fence without a covering. Only the true shepherd is admitted. See the flocks separate behind their own shepherd. "I know my sheep and am known of mine." The second scene is at noon. Picture the flock resting from the Eastern sun inside the rough enclosure. At the opening the shepherd stands. "I am the door." The third scene is at night, when darkness terrifies and dangers come. This is the time that the true shepherd shows his mettle: no mere hireling in time of danger, he is willing to die for his flock.

"The Lord is my shepherd, I shall not want."
What?
I shall not want *rest*, for
"He maketh me to lie down in green pastures."

I shall not want *drink*, for
"He leadeth me beside the still waters."

I shall not want *forgiveness*, for
"He restoreth my soul."

I shall not want a *guide*, for
"He leadeth me in the paths of righteousness for His name's sake."

27

I shall not want *companionship*, for
"Though I walk through the valley of the
shadow of death, I will fear no evil, for Thou
art with me."

I shall not want *comfort*, for
"Thy rod and Thy staff, they comfort me."

I shall not want *food*, for
"Thou spreadest a table before me in the
presence of mine enemies."

I shall not want *joy*, for
"Thou anointest my head with oil."

I shall not want *anything*, for
"My cup runneth over."

I shall not want *anything in this life*, for
"Goodness and mercy shall follow me all the
days of my life."

I shall not want *anything in the life to
come*, for
"I shall dwell in the house of the Lord for ever."

9

The Consistency of the Bible

LAST WEEK a subscriber wrote to the Editor as follows:

I am not looking for discrepancies or incompatibilities in the Scriptures, but here are two passages which I find it hard to reconcile:

"One generation passeth away, and another generation cometh: but the earth abideth for ever."—*Ecclesiastes 1 : 4.*

"Heaven and earth shall pass away, but my words shall not pass away."—*Matthew 24: 35.*

The writer of the Book of Ecclesiastes in his earlier mood is a world-weary cynic, who sits like a sick eagle on the branch of a tree and regards the world with a lack-lustre eye. To such a one the picture of the passing generations of men seems pathetic. They come and go, but the old earth on which they live goes on, gradually absorbing the ruins of other ages. But that reflection is only true from one point of view. We know perfectly well that the solar system and all the material universe changes. Stars burn out and new stars appear, and the whole universe is only important in the mind which can conceive it. The Moral Law, which reached its highest expression in the words of Christ, would still exist if our little world should pass away. The perplexity of our friend is chiefly important, not for the problem which it states, but because of a certain conception of the Scriptures which seems implied. What is the Bible?

It may be stated at once that the words of the Bible are not like arithmetic figures, which always mean the same. Let us look for a moment at the character and scope of the greatest Book in the world.

First of all, it is not a book, but a library. It is made up of sixty-six books which were written over a period of fifteen hundred years by authors of every kind. Some were scholars and some were uneducated men. The variety in the contents of the Bible is still more remarkable. We find here history, poetry, philosophy, epigrams, mystical visions, and some of the greatest stories in the world. There are portraits of saints, heroes, warriors, and scoundrels of the deepest dye. All this is obvious, and yet the most supreme quality of the Bible is a certain unity which is to be found in its pages from the beginning to the end. Let us mention only a few of the things which express the divine unity of the Book of Books.

First, it takes for granted that there is a spiritual background to the universe, and in this the Bible is more modern than many people suppose. "In the beginning God." Thirty years ago Arthur Balfour wrote, "We now know too much about matter to be materialistic," and the other day Professor Jeans said, "The universe seems to be nearer to a great thought than a great machine."

The second sign of unity in the Bible is that it assumes that there is a difference between right and wrong. In other words, it believes in the existence of sin. One of the most distinguished men of the Supreme Court of Canada was speaking in Toronto the other day about the spiritual landmarks in his own life, and he described a scene thirty years ago when Lord Morley received his honorary degree from the University of Toronto. As the famous biographer of William Gladstone rose, many of the young men expected a torrent of oratory, but the philosopher said to his young hearers: "There isn't very much really worth while to speak about. There are two things in life that are important: first, the difference between right and wrong, and, second, that every effect has its cause." The story of the Bible in many pictures describes right and wrong and shows how they affect the life of man.

The third characteristic to be found everywhere in the Bible is the doctrine of redemption. It is like a scarlet thread from Genesis to Revelation. If you cut a page anywhere, it will bleed. Redemption by personally leading up to the climax of human history when the Son of Man appeared among men.

Fourth, there is a sense of progress throughout the Book. No one expects that the saints and heroes before the days of Abraham should have the same spiritual conception of God as Isaiah and Amos. There is a very necessary doctrine to be found in the Bible, and that is that evolution is a two-lane road. It runs both ways. There is no assurance for the inevitable and automatic progress, either of nations or individual men; and yet, through it all, there is a confident faith in the purpose of the Creator.

The story of our race, as told in Genesis, begins in the Garden of Eden and it ends by the banks of the River of Life, in the New Jerusalem. The imagery of the last book in the Bible is taken from the first. The gold and precious stones and the river and the tree of life of the first Eden all appear in the second. The unity of the Bible transcends all textual criticism. It is the unity of life and the unity of God.

10

The Hunger of the Soul

Blessed are they which do hunger and thirst
after righteousness: for they shall be filled.
—*Matthew 5 : 6.*

WE HAVE VENTURED to call this Beatitude "The Hunger of
the Soul." When Laura Bridgman, who was deaf and
blind, was an inmate of Dr. Howe's asylum for the blind
at Boston, her teacher one day made some reference to
the soul. A look of bewilderment overspread the child's
face, and she slowly spelled out on her fingers the
question, "What is the soul?" "The soul," replied Dr.
Howe, "in the complicated language used not only by
teachers but preachers also, is that which thinks and feels
and hopes." A look of rare discernment mantled the
blind girl's face. "And is it," she immediately inquired
with eager fingers, "is it that which aches so?"

In Charnwood's "Life of Abraham Lincoln" there is a
story of the last days of the great President's life. As blind
men long for light, Lincoln groped after a fuller and
sweeter faith. He tried many of the gates by which other
pilgrims entered the City of Happiness, but wistfully he
was compelled, with a sad shake of the head, to turn
away. He said to a friend: "I have been reading the
Beatitudes, and can at least claim one of the blessings

therein unfolded. It is the blessing pronounced upon those who hunger and thirst after righteousness." It is the consolation prize for those who feel that the beatific and the martyr's crown are too high for them.

Hunger and thirst are signs of health. They prove that you are normal. When you go to see the doctor, one of the questions he asks is, "How is your appetite?" Loss of appetite is the red flag that nature hangs out to tell you that there is danger ahead.

A good appetite is a means of growth. The little baby in the cradle is a bundle of hungers and thirsts. He does not know what he wants, but he knows when he gets it. Not only so, but he lets the whole household know if he does not get it!

Hunger and thirst are a source of enjoyment. We are fond of speaking of "the bread that mother used to make." It must have been good, but perhaps one reason that we remember it is because of the appetite with which we were blessed when we were children. More than one faithful wife has grown grey before her time in an effort to coax the lagging appetites of some member of the family.

Perhaps there has never been a time when people frankly hungered and thirsted for pleasure as they do today. Any one who has eyes to see, and cares to use them, knows that with hundreds and thousands of people, young and old, self-gratification is the chief business of life. They put immense enthusiasm and boundless zeal into the pursuit, but, alas, happiness is one of the by-products of life. Those who make it their god are never satisfied. The jaded senses are flogged by unnatural stimulation till at last there is no response.

The Christian Church has not always agreed with the

teaching of Jesus as to what men live by. There is a fable told in the wonderful novel of Dostoevsky. In the days of the Inquisition Our Lord returned to earth. He was cast into prison and was visited by the Grand Inquisitor, who said to Him: "You have come back to spoil our work. In the wilderness the devil knew what men longed for, and he offered you those three things and you refused them—bread, authority and mystery. We have had to correct your work, or there would be no Church. You were advised to take bread as an instrument, because men will follow one who gives them bread. You were advised to make peace with the powers of the earth, because authority is necessary. You were advised to show some marvel that men might be astounded, because they would follow any one who can dazzle them. You were foolish enough to believe that men hunger and thirst for pure righteousness." The Grand Inquisitor was clever, but Jesus was wise.

11

The Christian Quadrilateral

ONE OF THE MOST SIGNIFICANT characteristics of our age is the lack of certainty in the minds of many people with regard to the accepted traditions of the past, and this is peculiarly true in the realm of religion. Any one who is willing to see must know that Christianity is fighting for its life today in a sense that it has not done for many centuries.

This is by no means an unmixed tragedy because the gospel of Christ is a crusade and a challenge to the heroic in the human spirit. In olden days, when the Austrian Empire dominated northern Italy, there were four cities which, because of their strength, were called the quadrilateral or four-square fortresses. Christianity has four impregnable fortresses within which the human spirit is safe from every storm that blows, and needs to fear no one.

The first fortress is the fact of Christian experience. There is nothing of which a man is more certain than what he has known in his inner life, and the gospel of Christ shows that very thing. Apart from the cosmic aspects of religion, there is the mystical quality which cannot be gainsaid. It brings consciousness of peace, it tells a man of the nearness of God, it assures him that his burdens will be carried for him by One who understands. It is a strange thing that the heart of all prayers is the same; whether rich or poor, all are on a level here. Different churches unite at the altar stairs that slope up to God. The writers of the great hymns are universal; the Roman Catholic, Anglican, the Greek and the Unitarian all speak the language of the heart. Religion is the greatest uniting influence between nations. Christians find their comradeship with those of another color in Jesus Christ.

The second fortress is the fact of the Church. By this we mean the blessed company of all faithful people everywhere. We are in danger of forgetting that fact. There is an unseen mystical church which embraces the true hearts in all the churches to which we belong. The persecutions of the churches of Germany today remind us that the Roman Empire tried to stamp out the church of God, but the Roman Empire is dead and the Church of Rome still remains. The Church lasts because ideally it is built on Jesus Christ. The fact of the Church is a phenomenon that no sophistry can talk away.

The third fortress is the Bible. It is a unique book. It has a message which is different from any other in the world—a library of over sixty volumes within one cover, written by men of all types and culture. Think of what it has done in literature. If the Bible were taken out of English literature, the greatest authors of our language would be unintelligible. In so far as it is possible for any human symbol to incarnate the Divine, the Bible is an impregnable fortress of the spirit.

This work remains for us today, as it did for our fathers in their day, the great light and inspiration of the ages. Its sound and practical admonitions for this life, its explanation of the mystery of life, its clue to the secrets of human existence, its hope for the future, its revelation of the being and character of God, and the destiny of man, stand today, in the midst of all the teeming literature of the world, unapproachable, incomparable, supreme.

The fourth fortress is the key of the fortification. It is the fact of Christ. This is the most important. This is the cause of the other three. Think of His life! Of all the millions and millions who have lived upon this earth He is the only sinless being, He is the contemporary of every generation. As the centuries roll by, the personality of the Saviour of mankind is more bright through the distance. Not only His life but His death is unique. The personality of Christ gives power and eternity to the conception of religion. The Rock of Ages is not a poetic fancy; it is an experience which has given hope and safety to a great portion of mankind.

12

The People and the Church

THE RECENT BROADCAST of the Archbishop of Canterbury, which he named "A Recall to Religion," was so reasonable and so serious that it must have caused many people throughout the Empire to consider his anxious and beautifully phrased appeal.

There is a great interest in religion, as he said, but it is also true that multitudes who have an interest in religion have drifted from the Christian Church, which is the one organization in the modern world which lives for religion. It is a serious situation when men who believe in Jesus Christ are cold to His Church. We do not think that a Churchless Christianity is desirable or in the long run possible. Therefore a recall to religion means a recall to the Church. But to what kind of Church can we recall men today? There is no doubt that the real trouble is with organized religion itself. It is because we are loyal to the Church we are jealous of any sign of failure. As a matter of fact, the world has made a far greater mess of its business than the Church ever made of hers. But "the worst is the sickness of the best," and the glorious ideal of the Bride of Christ is that she should be free from spot or stain or any such thing. We shall not ask anything which is not reasonably attainable in the Church in which we find ourselves today.

38

First, there is the age-long dream of a reunited Christendom, "That they may be all one." It is surely possible that every man, irrespective of race or nation or color, who is loyal to Christ the King, should keep the sense of unity in his heart, respect those who differ from him and pray and work for the fulfilment of our Lord's sacramental prayer. Too often the man on the street sees the various Churches as competing firms, trying to put one another out of business.

Second, the plain man asks that the Church should return to the simplicity of Christ. We waste energy in anxious attempts to make our faith scientific or modern or anything rather than the good news of redemption. Teach men the love of God and show them that man cannot attain the true stature of his glory till he knows God. Show him the Cross and the lesson that pain is part of life and that no Christian can find Christ and yet escape the experience of the Cross.

Third, the Church needs a braver demand in the matter of practice. Of all things in the world men seem to expect immediately to become skilled and able members of a Church once they join it. That is sheer nonsense. We need to learn to pray. There is too much exhortation and too little teaching, and in this the Roman Catholic Church is an example which others should emulate. Men should go to Church to worship, and not to be amused. Popular preaching may be a snare and the very people for whom it was provided casually fade away when it ceases to thrill. The Church can never compete with the movies.

Fourth, the Church members should cure that strange, furtive reluctance to explain their faith, if they have any. Surely there is something wrong in the essentially British custom of acting as if religion was something to be kept in a safety deposit box. Any woman will tell you why she likes a certain doctor or whether she prefers gas or electricity in the kitchen. You cannot keep the average man from telling you the good points of his new car. We, too, must be able to explain why, in a pagan world, we practice a certain religion.

Fifth, we must preach the Sermon on the Mount as a community which practices it. The world thinks that the Church preaches and prays one thing and the Institution proclaims another. The Church of Christ means more than a deepening of the spiritual life in the individual soul. It must involve the witness to a social order which will be an alternative to fascism and communism. Many who stand out of the Church do not do so because they are unchristian, but because they think, perhaps wrongly, that the Church is not Christian enough.

Finally, although it may seem a contradiction, the average man hates the idea that Christians exist to improve other people. The noblest title ever given to the Bishop of Rome was "Servus Dei Servorum"—the Servant of the Servants of God. That is like Christ. We are improved by God and by His grace. This age is intolerant of uplifters. The temper of our time is curiously suspicious of any sign of patronage or arrogance in any great historic institution, either secular or religious. It is a terrifying thought that the Divine message of salvation is committed to human hands. The Church has a great place in the world. She has done incredible things, and she will still reign in the hearts of men as long as she remembers her Master's words, "He that will be first among you, let him be the servant of all."

13

Is Anyone There?

No one who has ever attempted to wrestle with the greatest of all moral problems concerning the place of a personal God in this universe can be surprised that men, in their agony, have often cried out: "If there is a God, why does He not speak? Is He a person with a perverted sense of humor Who likes to conceal His autograph after the manner of the Baconian theory, so that suffering human beings must follow the trail which He has been pleased to leave in the labyrinth of nature?" Many of us have been haunted by the thought that if God wanted to reveal Himself to us, why did He not do so in a way that would make doubts and misunderstanding impossible? From one point of view it would seem plausible that the benevolent Creator of the universe, if He had a message which was all-important for mankind, should put it into a form that every one could believe and comprehend.

The answer to this problem may be found in another question: "How could God reveal Himself to us so all could recognize Him?" Perhaps the easiest method might seem to be some very striking miracle. According to our Christian history there was just such a miracle which happened one night on the Judean hills nearly two thousand years ago. All the drama and the romance that could be desired are in the story of the Nativity and the subsequent history of the Son of Man who lived and died by the Mediterranean Sea.

But a new difficulty comes to us. We see now that even the greatest miracle which happened in the past might easily be disputed by subsequent generations of men. It is their privilege and prerogative to doubt what they please and there is no means by which you can persuade the people of the twentieth century that a superhuman event occurred before the days of modern journalists and photographers.

So then it is necessary that the miracle should happen frequently in order that every one may see it. But, if this should come to pass, it would no longer be a miracle; it would be one of the ordinary routine incidents in this little side-show of ours on a second-class planet of the solar system. If God wrote a message on the sky, who could prove that it was God who wrote it?

As a matter of fact the only way in which God could show Himself beyond the possibility of doubt would be by compelling every mind to think in exactly the same way. But, if that should happen, we would be deprived of our freedom, and it is that gift of freedom which is part of the Divinity in our make-up which is our greatest charter of dignity in the scheme of things as they are.

No, when we are dealing with spiritual and non-material things the method of our learning and progress must be of a subtler kind. There is no moral or spiritual life where freedom is absent, and a man compelled to be good or religious is no longer a child of God; he is a puppet or a vegetable.

If God respects what we are led to believe is His highest creation, He must deal reverently with our freedom. He will not shout, but speak with the still small voice to our conscience, and, therefore, it does not seem surprising that God's voice comes to us in ways which do not beat us down but leave us the power to listen if we will.

The greatest purpose of revelation is not merely to give information, but it is to develop a power for communion with God. The spiritual life grows by what it feeds on, and the romance of the Incarnation reveals God's method of speech, for "the spirit of man is the candle of the Lord."

14

The Hopefulness of God

IN THESE DAYS it seems necessary to remind ourselves that the theologians have overlooked some of the attributes of God. In the past generations when men tried to put into human words a portrait of the Creator they very largely confined themselves to stating certain necessary characteristics of the Great Architect of the Universe, His sovereignty, His justice and, of course, His mercy and His love for His children.

In the morning of the world, when God joyously cast the stars into the sky, there was an invincible hope in the poem of creation. As each successive stage ended, "God saw that it was good." But was it? Just as everything in God is dark unless you set it in the atmosphere of love, so everything in history is " a tale told by an idiot" unless we can see in our human story the hopefulness of God.

Let us look at the ways of God with men. From one point of view there is a merciless and impersonal element in nature which makes man in certain moods shrink from its coldness and severity. We cannot fathom it. But, just as everything that man has never touched has a beauty of its own, it also has its hope which must have come from the Source of all things. Every seed thrown in the ground is kissed with the hope of harvest. Every bird sings as it makes its nest. The Voice that breathed o'er Eden is the overture to every wedding. Every river laughs on the mountain side as it begins its run toward the sea, in spite of Henley's mournful picture. St. Paul, in a celebrated passage, talks of all creation groaning and travailing in pain, but the very metaphor he uses is that of the most hopeful event in human life—the birth of a child into the world.

This is evident in the spirit of the New Testament. From the song of the Angels of Bethlehem and the Magnificat to the final vision of the New Jerusalem, the story of the Bible is a song of hope. The Gospels and the Epistles take no hopeless view of the future of humanity. They are the most glowing literature in the world.

Jesus Christ is the greatest of all optimists. With a vision that the frailty of man could never darken He saw all that was worst in the human heart. There is a maddening cheerfulness that ignores reality. This was not the hopefulness of our Saviour. He was gloriously hopeful till He conquered death—hopeful for Mary Magdalene, hopeful for Peter, hopeful for the future of the world, "Lo, I am with you alway." Any man who has heard the words "He that hath seen Me hath seen the Father" can never doubt the hopefulness of God.

Immortality is God's greatest gift of hope to mankind. Sheer materialism can end only in the blankest despair. What real use is man's work if he perishes? If the end of every race and every individual is to be annihilation, what then? . . .

A time will come when the planets will be the charnel house of all living things and gradually cool into a frozen block. The end of man upon this earth, the end of all his toil and tears and prayers, the end of all his striving for knowledge and beauty will be but a universal grave.

Without the hopefulness of God, that is all that lies before us.

But man is God's poem, His dream and His experiment. But it cannot be worked out in threescore years and ten. For the Divine human drama a stage of Eternity is necessary.

And so amid the shadows of our age of pessimism let every man who remembers that the spirit of man is the candle of the Lord hear Christ's words through the centuries, "Be ye therefore perfect"—and so he sets out on the eternal quest.

> *"He asks no isles of the blest,*
> *No quiet seats of the just,*
> *To rest in a golden grave*
> *Or to bask in a summer sky;*
> *Give him the glory of going on and not to die."*

15

The Ethics of Pain

THE PROBLEM OF PAIN is as old as human existence. The Book of Job is one of the oldest and noblest things ever written by man, and yet it fails to answer the question, Why?

Speaking broadly, past generations of religious men accepted the facts of human existence and even questioned whether it was right for man to think of changing the conditions of his brief dwelling on this planet.

Since the birth of our scientific age we have done so much to eliminate famine, disease and other evils that the world has begun to expect a painless world. It may be useful for us to consider the Christian view of trouble and sorrow.

To begin, we might just as well admit that life is essentially difficult and tragic. A great many people begin by thinking that the ideal life is normal, making the fatal mistake of looking at all adversity as a personal insult to themselves. But if we begin by accepting life as "a thing to try the soul's stuff upon," then all the blessings, joy and love that enrich us will appear a miracle of beauty.

Christianity also teaches us that it is an honor to be able to suffer. Long ages ago some creatures, like the turtle and the oyster, had the bright idea of pulling their skeletons outside and keeping their nervous system inside that they might avoid pain. But that was the road to darkness and death.

Later in the story of life a new theory grew which put the skeleton inside and the tingling nerves near the surface. All the beauty and goodness of man would have been impossible unless he were sensitive to joy and pain. The life of Christ is full of this idea. He was the Great Sufferer so that what happened to His brethren happened also to Him. In our deepest moments, we know the education of pain.

> *I walked a mile with Pleasure,*
> *She chattered all the way*
> *But left me none the wiser*
> *For all she had to say.*

> *I walked a mile with Sorrow,*
> *And ne'er a word said she;*
> *But, oh, the things I learned from her*
> *When Sorrow walked with me.*

There is more thinking going on in Canada now about the possibility of a decent world than in happy, careless days. "No one thinks till he has to."

Injustice has its compensations—a world where the innocent suffer. It is true that the natural world is hard and relentless, but never malicious. It takes man to reach that state of infamy. But it is also true that the finest things in life come because justice is blind. Who would live in a world without adventure? Who would have a history written without one word about the heroes and madmen who have glorified the human name because they never served for pay?

Our world is so made that our greatest gifts are our

48

greatest sorrows and our mistakes are a stepping stone to immortality. This does not mean that we do not rebel against injustice. The Strange Man on His cross cried out in the darkness, My God, Why? Why?

The story of the making of a pearl is a parable that all may read. Somehow a grain of sand or some other foreign substance enters the shell of the oyster on the ocean floor of the Persian Gulf. It cannot be ejected; it is an irritation that becomes in time, because it is inevitable, a gem.

It is a great mistake to think that trouble tends to drive men away from God. Religion and trouble are twins. Travail means that a birth is near, and the child of sorrow is faith and love.

The problems of pain that drive us mad are those caused by man himself. God is not responsible for him because He gave man something of Himself—the power to choose right or wrong.

But the universe is friendly. The stars have no malice, though they shine with a cold light. Faith gives man the power to transmute his sorrow into joy.

16

I Hate Lent

MANY, NO DOUBT, AGREE with the words of Dean Swift, who wrote: "I hate Lent. I hate different diets and furmity and butter and herb porridge, and sour faces of people who only put on religion for seven weeks." If Lent means that, you certainly do hate it; you hate Lent because it is a bore and a nuisance, a sort of moral manicure in which you trim off the edges of frivolity. But Lent is more than that. In the first place, Lent is a very definite technique for dealing with sin.

A few years ago Sir Oliver Lodge said that the world had forgotten sin. Certainly the modern world was doing everything imaginable to make man believe that he needed no redemption. We have become wiser through sorrow and disaster. Our modern rationing has taught us, against our will, that it is a good thing for a man or a nation to starve the body to save the soul. We are in the mood this Ash Wednesday to go further and admit that as individuals and as a people we need the forgiveness and the help of God. For God has other words for other worlds, but for this world the word of God is Christ.

Thoughtful people are realizing that the most urgent need for our day is a return to the fundamentals of religion. Our spiritual bankruptcy in a time of world distress—the sense of inadequacy so many of us feel in handling our personal problems—are evidences of soul sickness as well as economic maladjustment. It is not the clergy alone who are saying this. Far weightier is the testimony of bankers, statesmen and business men, who say that civilization cannot survive without the reinforcement of religion. Obviously religion is no magic remedy in a few painless doses. It is no easy way out for any of us. The practice of religion involves the same expenditure of time and effort as the cultivation of any great art. Vital religion cannot be had on easy terms with no down payment. It involves sacrificial living and painful effort. No proxies are acceptable. Every man must draw his own breath. Every person must nourish his own soul.

Second, Lent is facing the cross. And it is in this season that we see what the cross is made of. It is made not of wood, but of sin upon sin and shame upon shame, that add up to a total tragedy of malignity and stupidity. The head of the cross is not of wood. The head of the cross is a class of pious, narrow folk who think they are better than they are and despise others. The body of the cross is not of wood. The body of the cross is a crowd made up of a callous mob and a little band of cowardly friends, including ourselves. The right arm of the cross is Pilate and his gospel of political expediency. The left arm is just common treachery in the person of Judas. And there is something of us in the head, the body and the arms of that cross. And it was upon that cross that Jesus was crucified. That's the cross we face this Lent. Now then, hate Lent, but hate first all the sin that Lent recalls, and the cross to which it led.

Lent recalls us from the market-place or the counting-house, the scene of pleasure, or it may be the ties of home, and bids us think of the mystery of life, Divine and

51

human, of God and ourselves, and what we ought to be and do for one another, and what our destiny is and what God's will is for the world. Lent is not merely or mainly a season of special rules or exercises; it is rather an opportunity to gain a more effective motive to carry us forward to the tasks of our discipleship. That motive is penitence. If it begins by taking us into the wilderness, it is to bring us to Him who shows us how we too may conquer in our hour of temptation. If it ends in the darkness of the Cross, it is that we may share the triumph of Easter.

> *Breathes there a man who claimeth not*
> *One lonely spot,*
> *His own Gethsemane,*
> *Whither with his inmost pain*
> *He fain*
> *Would weary plod,*
> *Find the surcease that is known*
> *In wind a-moan*
> *And sobbing sea,*
> *Cry his sorrow hid of men,*
> *And then—*
> *Touch hands with God.*

17

Battle in the Desert

A TRAVELLER IN PALESTINE, long ago, said that there were four things in the Holy Land which never changed. First, the stars, looking down with shining eyes as they did on the night of Calvary. Secondly, the Canyon of the Jordan—the strange river that runs from Mount Hermon down to the salt waters of the Sodomitic Sea. The mountains are the same as they were when Moses looked down on the Promised Land; and lastly, the heart of man is still the same.

The Lenten season is fashioned from that strange, mystic event known as Our Lord's temptation. The place is one of the mountains of which we have spoken called Quarantania, over the Dead Sea above Jericho, a place of incredible desolation where the Son of Man fasted among the wild beasts. The time is very significant. Dripping from the fords of Jordan, with His Father's benediction ringing in His ears, like Christian with his new armor from the House Beautiful, who went straight to the Valley of Humiliation in the "Pilgrim's Progress" to meet Appolyon, Christ goes to the desert hill for His vigil. In modern terms, it is like the parade of the battalion with the music of the band and the flags flying, and two days later, in the trenches, amid the shells. This is human life.

It is a mistake to think that temptation always comes with well-advertised preparation. Its danger lies in the fact that it catches us off guard in an unexpected hour.

When is a young man's danger? Is it not very often at the time of exaltation, in the moment of his conscious strength, when he feels the mystery of his power? Remember that Elijah, the greatest of all the Prophets, after his thrilling victory on Mount Carmel, when he vindicated God before the assembled thousands of Israel and finished in a burst of glory, by leading Ahab's chariot eighteen miles across the plain to the gates of Jezreel, in a moment of reaction fled before the wild words of an angry woman and lay down under a juniper tree, wishing that he were dead.

It is a significant thing that in the great moments of life man is alone. We are alone at birth and alone at death, and, in this great moment, the Son of Man who loved His fellowmen fought His battle with the tempter without a friend at His side. It is touches like these from the Gospel story which make us understand that Christ was our brother.

The old theologians used to worry as to whether Christ was "not able to sin" or "able not to sin," but the whole meaning of the Incarnation is that it was a real temptation. Our Redeemer was not an angel, flying over the tree-tops of life, but a man, walking on a stony road. Millions who would lose sight of the angel will gladly follow the Man.

We have said that the temptation was real. Whether it was subjective or objective does not matter. Three great imaginative artists have tried to picture the scene in different ways. To Milton the tempter was a hermit in the desert; and, by the way, it is rather remarkable that

54

Milton, who in "Paradise Lost" so gloriously pictures the fall of man, failed in "Paradise Regained" when he tried to paint the temptation. The reserve of Scripture is beautiful and wise.

Bengel rather suggests that the tempter was an emissary of the Sanhedrin, and a French painter, in a striking manner, depicts the personality of Satan as a shadow of Christ Himself, in the background. If we had been there we might have seen the weary, meditative figure of Christ with nothing else visible to human eye except the circling eagle in the sky and the flitting of some desert animal passing beneath the hill.

But it was real; otherwise it has no business in the Gospel story. Whatever it does, this dramatic scene reveals Jesus battling for His own soul, even as you and I. If Jesus did not fight His own devil, as we do, His example means very little to humanity. The One who would help us by His example must stand on our ground.

Some people are almost startled at the thought that Christ could be tempted. Shakespeare says a very beautiful thing in "Measure for Measure": "It is one thing to be tempted, Escalus; another thing to fall."

18

Stones and Bread

THE THREE TEMPTATIONS rise on an ascending scale from
the lowest instincts of man to the highest dreams of the
soul. Our Lord was absorbed for days in meditation and
thought of His divine mission, and, as men have ever
been under circumstances of intense concentration, He
felt no need of food, and at last He awoke to feel Himself
starving.

Do you know what it is to be hungry? Not half an
hour late for lunch, but the real savage hunger of
elemental man. Such hunger has changed the history of
the world. It sent the Goths and Mongols rolling in
waves to swamp the most ancient civilizations, and it may
do so again.

To any one who has never seen the land of Palestine,
the multitude and variety of stones are incredible, and in
the desert there are flat oval stones very much like the
cakes which the Mother of Jesus must have made in the
outdoor oven at Nazareth. Therefore it was perfectly
natural that the thought should come to the Redeemer,
"Why not use your divine power? There surely can be
no harm in that. After all, a dead prophet is not much
good to the world."

It is suggested also That He "was with the wild beasts,"

in the words of St. Mark. There could be no fitter companions for Him at that moment. They represented rapacious and unhallowed power, whose only motive was passion and the indulgence of desire uncontrolled by reason or pity, and so the first temptation was to decide whether Christ's power should be hallowed or unhallowed—like that of God or the wild beasts.

We may ask ourselves the question then, Why did Jesus refuse to make the stones into bread? The chief reason was because of you and me. For one day when we were sore pressed, the word of God might have come to us saying, "Do not surrender. Do not sell your soul for your stomach." If Jesus had not conquered this temptation, we would have been perfectly justified in replying: "It's all very well for You, but when You trod the earth You did not hesitate to use the special gifts of God to help You out of a tight corner. You only pretend to know what humanity has to endure. No one can be my Saviour who will perform a little private miracle for himself." It would have finished Jesus Christ for you and for me.

And so it was that the siliceous rocks which were commonly called "Elijah's Melons" were allowed to remain unchanged.

It is very interesting to notice how Jesus resists temptation. He tells us what man's life is. "Man shall not live by bread alone." After all, what is our life? Sometimes it may mean that which keeps the physical structure alive. Sometimes life may more truly mean the ideal schooling of the human mind. To the moralist life means the choice of what is right rather than what is wrong, and the stern path of duty. Sometimes it rises to the mystical conception of spiritual longing contained in the words of St. Augustine, "O God, Thou hast made us for Thyself, and our hearts can find no rest until they rest in Thee."

"Blessed is the man or the church that is strong enough never to put bread away, however sweet it be to the hungry lips, if, by tasting it, he robs himself of the nourishment of the higher life." Here Jesus spoke for the whole human race whose lot He assumed. Is there anything in life beyond the blubber and pewter spoons and a gramophone, which an Eskimo in Coronation Gulf once chose as his conception of perfect bliss? One of the great stories of English literature is the faith of Captain Robert Scott and his companions in the flimsy slackened tent on the frozen wastes of the Antarctic as they returned in 1912 from the South Pole. The glorious message which he wrote to Sir James Barrie will never be forgotten: "Their bodies lie in a sepulchre of ice. The drifting snow sings a requiem over their cairn, but their names are immortal, for they scorned safety, ease and comfort, and their example will kindle the eyes of schoolboys yet unborn." It is a modern interpretation of the First Temptation.

19

Sensation and Religion

WE LEFT JESUS TRIUMPHANT at the end of the first round
with the Tempter, but Satan comes back. "Not by bread
but by trust." "Ah," says the devil. "Our hero is in a
religious mood. We will play upon it, then. He shall
have a religious temptation this time."

Milton in his "Paradise Regained" attempts to paint the
scene. It is on the pinnacle of the temple in the Holy
City. The exact spot was on the Stoa Basilike, or the royal
porch on the southern side of the temple overlooking the
Kedron. "There, on the highest pinnacle, he set the Son
of God." What a wonderful opportunity to gather a
crowd. You can imagine the great yards of the temple in
the middle of the day crowded with people as curious
then as they are now if a steeplejack appears on King
Street on the top of St. James'. What fool is that on the
steeple? Look at him. He is like a spider on a sunbeam.
It positively makes me dizzy. He will fall. Heavens, he
has jumped!

Was there ever such a sensation? But the Prophet of
Nazareth lands like a feather on His toes, and bowing
like a juggler, he is the great religious sensation since
Elijah overwhelmed the priests on Carmel. You can
imagine the movie-picture machines if they had had them
in those days. Who can it be? "I am Jesus of Nazareth,
the prophet of God."

59

This picture needs very little elaboration but nevertheless there are certain thoughts which come to our minds. In the first place here is the presumption of the Son of God who has laid aside His divinity to walk the ways of man. To one of us it would be no temptation to jump from the Dome of St. Peter's or the Eiffel Tower, but Jesus knew that His Father would not let him fall, and therefore He was renouncing his Incarnation. We can see the subtlety of Satan preaching the gospel of trust. "You say you trust God for everything. How splendid! Now prove it." And we ourselves in our own degree are forbidden to presume on God's love for us. Here is the danger to Christian people who think that their religion ought to exempt them from everything. Job gives us the true answer, "Though He slay me, yet will I trust Him."

In the second place we are reminded that God does not countenance sensational methods in religious teaching. The period near the time of Christ was filled with prophets who were charlatans and wonder workers. Apollonius of Tyana was one, Demonax was another, and the Apocryphal Gospel of Thomas with its childish and vindictive miracles attributed to Jesus, which reveal him as a precocious and rather bad-tempered boy, show us the danger of trying to imitate the inspired word of God. And even today there are signs that in modern life so-called Christian teachers do not hesitate to use cheap sensation to draw people to Church. There are ludicrous and blasphemous sermon titles to be found among the Church notices in many cities of the English-speaking world. It is a dangerous thing for the preacher of the gospel of Christ to attempt to compete with Hollywood. Man's appetite for marvels is insatiable. Facilis descensus Averni.

Every honest man will confess that during His earthly life Jesus never worker any deed of wonder in order to paralyze mankind. Every miracle of His was only performed from pity for human needs. Jesus, the prophet of Galilee, came to tell man of God and God's love. The only legitimate argument for truth is that it is true. Christ once referred rather cryptically to some one who wanted a marvel, to the sign of the Prophet Jonah; and what was that? Simply a stranger, tattered and dripping with sea water, without credentials, preaching passionately the Son of Man and the mercy of God. Christ could not be an ignoble conjurer, even for God. He came to preach salvation for its own pure sake. "Get thee behind me, Satan."

20

The Empire of Christ

WE HAVE SAID that the three temptations appeal in succession to the lower, higher and highest nature of man. The third temptation is almost glorious in its audacity and Miltonic horizon. It is Satan's last word. He took the Saviour to the top of an exceedingly high mountain and showed Him all the glory and the wonder of the earth, and these were his words: "All these things will I give Thee if Thou wilt fall down and worship me."

The words of the temptation, which could only have come from the lips of Christ, have a childlike simplicity and glamour. We sometimes forget that Jesus of Nazareth was a country boy, that He spent His years in the Town of Nazareth, like an eagle's nest in the Galilean hills. On the rock above the town, looking down on Mary's well, Jesus must often have looked westward to the Mediterranean Sea, where in the distance He saw the ships of Tyre sailing on their lawful occasions toward Gibraltar and Byzantium. Looking down toward the Plain of Ezdraelon, He saw the highway from Egypt to Babylon, and many a day the little Boy saw the caravans of camels with their mystic burdens plowing through the dust until they disappeared from view. And that was all He ever saw of foreign lands. He never went beyond Mount Hermon. His knowledge of the kingdoms of the earth and the glory of them was very much like our knowledge of the new Jerusalem. We wonder what the kingdoms were which Satan caused to pass before the eyes of Christ. Was it only the Mediterranean world of the Roman Empire? Was there any thought of India, or China, which was then a great nation? Was it possible that the future civilizations of the undiscovered America ever came into the mind of the tempted One? And whispering in His ear these words seemed to come, "Do you see that little hill with the gaunt cross on it? That is the only throne that You will ascend if You are not reasonable. All I want is a recognition, a mere acknowledgment of fact, and You can have the kingdoms of the world and be welcome to them, provided that You are realist enough to know that I cannot be ignored."

The battle is set. Would Christ compromise? That is one of the questions that His Church has not yet been able to answer finally. Three hundred years later, after the young Christian Church, fighting with no weapons but the spirit, had survived the ten great persecutions and emerged from the Catacombs to supersede the Roman Empire, the compromise of Constantine changed the whole direction of Christianity. Until that time it had been the religion of a minority which took no responsibility for the sins of the world, the flesh or the devil, but ever since that date the Church of Jesus Christ has consented tacitly to play the game of civilization, and it seems that it must continue to do so.

But in this picture Jesus apparently must have all or nothing. He refuses to compromise. Understood properly, the inevitable result of a cavalier's salute to Satan would have meant the renunciation of the Cross. From the very beginning of His ministry, the shadow of the Cross rises

63

behind the Son of Man. The voice of the tempter was answered on the Mount of the Transfiguration when Jesus set His face to go to Jerusalem. It must have been a hard thing to do. The voice of the tempter was probably not threatening, but very gentle and very low: "Why die and suffer for man? Bend just a little. They are not worthy of Your sacrifice."

21

The Second Watch

OUR LORD, IN SPEAKING to His disciples with that clairvoyant insight which is to be found in all His teaching, emphasizes the importance of the Second Watch. He is warning men that the soul must always be alert and ready, because the great moment may come at any time.

In olden ages the days and nights were divided into watches. This tradition has lived on in seamen's language and in the organization of military guards. We see a sentinel going on duty in the dark when the rest of the world is asleep. Let us think of the characteristics of the Second Watch of the night.

It is the lonely hour:

> "The night has a thousand eyes,
>   The day but one,
>   Yet the light of the bright world dies
>   With the dying sun."

It is the hour when vitality is low. Life is never at its fullest then. Ask the nurse in the sickroom who dreads that hour lest the patient may not survive the mystery of darkness.

It is the hour when nothing seems to happen. We never hear of it again in the New Testament, for it was the First Watch when the Saviour healed the sick by the lake shore at eventide, and it was the Third Watch when He walked on the waters just before daybreak.

It is the same with us. During the early evening there are footfalls on the street and there are lights in the windows. In the Third Watch of a Toronto night the milkman's wagon rumbles along, but it is during the Second Watch that the policeman is suspicious of light and sound.

This is a parable of our human life. The romance of youth is over. The impossible dreams have not come true. The strap of the pack is chafing the shoulder, and the step has lost its spring, and yet it is the time when man's best work is done—a long road on the plateau of life's island after we have climbed up from the sea, the dusty, monotonous challenge of those middle years: "Carry on." "Forward; and forward with them, draw my soul into time's sea. And to be glad or sad I care no more. But to have, and to have been before I cease to be."

Now is the time for songs of the night and faith comes into its own. "Thou shalt not be afraid for the terrible night; for He shall give His angels charge over thee to keep thee in all thy ways." The Christian man should not regret the coming of the testing hours. All the dreams and exuberance of youth are a preparation for the short span of maturity and power for which he was born. The long eventide of age, should it be granted, will be sweeter for this Second Watch—and then there will be another day.

The same truth holds good in history. For instance, the First Watch of the first night of another great war has just ended. It began last September after a stormy sunset of the unavailing hopes of mankind.

Our Christian King, in his message to the Empire,
66

suggested that the new year might be dark and that the comforting hand of God would be safer than any known way. The excitement of national dedication is over. The great decision is made, and now there comes the long waiting which is not easy for the soul. Now is the time for Christians to renew their strength. The glorious words at the conclusion of the Fortieth Chapter of Isaiah imply that we need not only spiritual speed but stamina. "They shall run, and not be weary: and they shall walk, and not faint."

So let us keep our vigil:

> "Though the night be dark and dreary,
>   Darkness cannot hide from Thee.
> Thou art He who, never weary,
>   Watchest where Thy people be."

22

Forgiveness

OF ALL THE PETITIONS in the Lord's Prayer there is none which seems to contradict the philosophy of modern life more than the request for forgiveness. In the first place, for the last thirty years we have been hearing from all kinds of pseudo-philosophers that the word "sin" is an archaic conception, dating back to the superstition of unenlightened man; that everything we do, if we are natural, can be explained by the reactions of our physical microcosm, and, still further, that it is not only right but our duty through self-expression (whatever that may mean) to fulfil our lives. Have you ever heard any one say this: "Can an individual act otherwise than he does? Taking into account temperament, education, environment, can any one be called a free agent? Is not sin destiny?" Here is a problem too great to settle finally. Nevertheless, whatever may come to him, the higher man can step out of this kingdom of cause and effect into another and a nobler realm. He can even face God directly and say, "I am not the man that I ought to be." If you don't like to hear this from the pulpit, you can find it in the greatest literature of antiquity. In the Orestes of Aeschylus we have a picture of the remorse of the hero who has murdered his mother. Even though he has been exonerated by his friend, by the chorus and by the oracle, nevertheless the majesty of conscience sweeps sophistry away. "I am guilty," he says. "I cannot beat down the conviction in my soul that I have sinned."

The second objection to sin takes the form of optimism. A young man says: "I didn't come into this world to fight a perpetual losing battle against overwhelming odds. Was not Nietzsche right after all when he said that a healthy mind digests sin just as easily as a healthy stomach digests Limburger cheese?" But this attitude of mind is not humanity at its best. There come moments to us all when we recognize only two entities, God and our own souls. We fling ourselves instinctively on the world's great altar stairs that slope through darkness up to God. All literature and history, the teaching underlying the human sacrifices, self-tortures, fetish worship and priestly tyranny are a proof of man's incurable conscience.

Our modern idea that sin is only a private business is entirely foreign to the spirit of Christianity. We do not say that it would be impossible to find God in a sinless world, but our knowledge of Him would not be nearly so clear or our love for Him so great. That is one aspect of the fact of sin in the world.

The Bible has much to say about forgiveness. The old Prophets of Israel were at their finest when they spoke of the character of a righteous God in relationship to forgiveness. "Though your sins be as scarlet, they shall be as white as snow. Though they be red like crimson, they shall be as wool." That is God forgiving divinely by blotting out and forgetting. But in the New Testament the teaching of Jesus shows that God does not forgive by forgetting but by giving. God did not forgive because Christ died, but Christ died to show how God forgives. The inscription round the Cross in St. Paul's Cathedral has this perfectly—"Sic Deus dilexit mundum," God so loved the world. When you go to God for forgiveness you get much more than anything you expected. You come away singing. That is the meaning of Divine Absolution.

There is something about forgiveness which makes every man try to dodge it if he can. The reason is that when men forgive they generally leave a stigma of humiliation—a barb in the stricken heart that remains forever. "She forgave him," as a writer in a modern novel said, in a study of marriage. "She forgave him but she kept him at arm's length." There was no "giveness" in her forgiveness. He preferred ruin, to her profound and indignant surprise, for she had been rather pleased with herself. We do not really know what forgiveness is until we look at the Cross.

23

The Little Hills

THERE ARE SOME GREAT MOUNTAINS in the world which are symbols of the majesty of the Creator, and there is no doubt that they have an influence on human character. The Himalayas, the Andes, the Alps and the Rockies belong to all mankind. In picture and in story they are part of the legend of our race, but they are so great that they become impersonal. To stand by the track of the Canadian National Railways and gaze on the fortress shape of Mount Robson simply dwarfs human personality.

In Palestine there are two such towering peaks—Mount Hermon in the north, and Sinai across the desert. They represent the cosmic forces of the universe and, like the stars, they speak of God far away. This is the message of the Old Testament.

But Jerusalem is surrounded by little hills, so small that a man may get to know and to love them. A Frenchman, Stendhall, said that the whole history of France might have been different if there had been hills on the horizon of Paris.

Yes, the soul of man needs its little hills—to stand like candlesticks when the light of life burns low.

That is what the New Testament does. It never attempts to prove that there is a God. That is taken for granted, but it shows us that there is not only power but tenderness—that the little hills are the hands of the mountains, and that God can make them small enough that we may see them and explore them.

We have learned lately that there are health and joy in our little hills around Toronto. The development of skiing has transformed the Canadian winter for our city dwellers. It may have a spiritual value in that it proves the climbs of life are compensated by the slide.

The site of the Temple is the most striking feature of the topography of Jerusalem—a level plateau half a mile square, in the centre of the city. Here, long ago, was the legendary mount Moriah where Abraham offered Isaac. Here, for a thousand years, stood in succession the Temples of Solomon, Zerubbabel and Herod, and the Mosque of Omar has crowned the site since Moslem conquered Palestine. Within the dome is a walled space where the living rock is the only visible thing, the old Altar of Sacrifice in the ancient Temple—a little hill of praise and prayer, the symbol of the spiritual in man's existence.

Every city needs its Temple, and so does the life of each one of us.

Just across the Kedron from the Temple there is a sloping hill that must have been in early days the Park of Jerusalem. It is on the eastern side, and over its shoulder runs the old Jericho road down to the canyon of Jordan. "Hither Jesus resorted many times with His disciples.

It is the Garden of Gethsemane which gives this hill its immortality. To describe it were desecration, but the very name is an invitation and a challenge.

The poet Gray sings that "the paths of glory lead but to the grave," but there is something here which suggests that the path of the grave leads to glory. Have you a Gethsemane?

> *Breathes there a man who claimeth not*
>   *One lonely spot,*
>   *His own Gethsemane,*
> *Whither with his inmost pain*
> *He fain*
>   *Would weary plod,*
> *Find the surcease that is known*
> *In mind a-moan*
>   *And sobbing sea,*
> *Cry his sorrow hid of men,*
> *And then—*
>   *Touch hands with God.*

The traditional site of the hill of Calvary goes back to about 320 A.D., when Helena, the mother of Constantine, came to find the holy places. A small church was erected then, and the present Church of the Holy Sepulchre was built by the Crusaders. Perhaps it does not matter where the exact spot was. When the whole world wanted to know, Jerusalem had been a deserted village for two centuries.

On Calvary we have the amazing spectacle of a suffering God, and in His suffering we find the springs of our forgiveness. We ought never to grow coldly accustomed to this wonderful news. Calvary ought to throw us into new surprises every time we see it, and every time we hear its story. God weeping is more wonderful than God speaking. God suffering is far more awful than God punishing. God on the Cross is infinitely more amazing than God on the throne.

73

There is a hill in Jewry,
Three crosses pierce the sky.
On the midmost He is dying
To save all those who die—
A little hill, a kind hill
To souls in jeopardy.

24

Thoughts About Evil

IT IS PROBABLE that the sum total of evil in the world is no greater than it has always been, but at the present time it is impossible to look upon this phenomenon, which has been the bane of human life, as tolerantly as in ordinary days. Many thinking men and women of the last generation did not believe in the innateness of evil. The nineteenth century, especially, was very optimistic. Our fathers had almost come to think that evil was a by-product of circumstance. It was hoped that when poverty, starvation and ignorance had been removed something like a millennium might ensue. Since the beginning of this war it is difficult to believe this. We are learning that cruelty, brutality and hate are very real things, with some independent origin of their own. It is therefore worth our while to consider this problem. There are three explanations which may be offered.

The first is that the universe had no design. It is a purely material thing. It may have happened by accident when somebody or something started a ball rolling, which went on producing what we call life, and which will some time smash to pieces at the end of an aimless journey. Fifty years ago this was a popular theory, but in recent times it has been outgrown. It might be said that a person who held this view would consider the word

"God" to mean "whatever the universe happens to be going to do next."

The second answer is suggested by various ideas of evolution. Generally speaking, the theory would seem to be that the universe was originally unconscious, but became creative as it went along, developing real novelties in its progress. God, therefore, is only the purpose of the universe, which somehow evolved Him, and vainly strives after a spiritual ideal which sprang from itself. God is not transcendent, but immanent. He is wholly within the universe. Therefore, as Dean Inge has pointed out, He shares the fate of the universe, whatever that may be.

The third choice is the view which has commended itself to the great majority of mankind. It teaches that God is outside and prior to all the world, and that He has created everything according to some plan. Of course this is Christian doctrine. The most serious difficulty in this conception of life is the existence of suffering and evil. When we look at the misery in the toiling of the human race and in the lower reaches of nature, which are reddened by tooth and claw, are we really going to maintain that *this* was designed by wisdom? Sometimes when we look at the bloody muddle on this planet, and we use those words literally, we could almost imagine that the Deus ex machina was a satirist. We are perfectly aware of the Christian explanation that God, when He made man, gave him free will and breathed in his nostrils the breath of life, and that therefore, unless man is to be deprived of his divinest faculty, he must take the consequences of his mistakes. This bright suggestion at first seems satisfactory, but when we think a little further we are still disturbed, because, if God is all-wise, He should have known the danger of giving man freedom, and although He may not be the Creator of pain and evil it was He who was responsible for the conditions which introduced them into a world which otherwise would never have known them; and if God did not know, because the universe is free to develop as it pleases, we are in doubt as to the future.

We have given three distinct views as to the meaning of evil. They come from the natural thinking of mankind. In the last of the alternatives we get some hint of the Christian conception of things. After all, Christianity lives by faith, and it draws upon sources of power which are not to be found elsewhere. In conclusion it may be said that there are certain things to which those who follow Christ must cling in all the darkness and doubt of our modern scene. We will mention only three. We must insist that the origin of evil is utterly remote from God, and again we believe that the origin of evil is veiled in impenetrable mystery. For instance, the existence of Satan is no answer, because we want to know who created him. And, finally, we must deny that there is anything in the world such as equal dualism; that is to say that, although good and evil do exist together, there is a bias toward righteousness which must win in the end. "God must reign till He hath put all enemies under His feet."

25

Calvary

As GOOD FRIDAY APPROACHES, an inner voice seems to be calling to every Christian: "Take off thy shoes from off thy feet, for the place whereon thou standest is holy ground." For as often as we draw near in spirit to the place that is called Calvary, we must needs confess: "This is none other than the House of God and this is the Gate of Heaven."

Calvary is a Latin word and is found only once in the Bible. It is a very little hill even in Palestine, where the mountains, except Hermon, would not be noticed in the range of the Canadian Rockies. And yet this was the magnet which drew Europe during two hundred years when the Crusades were the chief feature of history, and a little more than twenty years ago Allenby fulfilled a dream of centuries when Jerusalem fell into Christian hands. During this week, in spite of the war, thousands of pilgrims will be gathered near the sacred spot. Let us for a moment think of its significance.

It is a remarkable fact of which many are not aware that nearly one-third of the four Gospels is devoted to the story of the death of Christ. It may surprise some who make little of the Cross to confront this fact. In the history of Alexander the Great, Napoleon, or any other hero, the account of the death is merely an incident. But in some strange way the writers of the Gospels felt that the drama of the Crucifixion was unique. Perhaps no Christian who ever lived has had a greater influence on Christianity than St. Paul, but there is no mention of his death in the New Testament because it never occurred to any one that his passing was an event of supreme importance. Doubtless his dust mingles with the dust of Rome, hidden beneath the debris of the centuries. He holds his place, and it is a very noble place, among the martyrs of mankind, but when he died his work was done. But every one of the Apostles and writers of the New Testament seems convinced that the Cross is the central figure of Christianity. We may be permitted as it rises on the horizon to ask what it means.

The origin of the symbol which gives significance to Calvary comes from the sewers of humanity at its worst. What tyrant was it who first conceived the idea of nailing criminals to a tree? In the shadowed ages before the thing entered into history, some Eastern monster, drunk with cruelty, thought out this plan to prolong the agony of his enemies. The Carthaginians, from whom the Romans learned the practice, were a very cruel race. In fact, until Jesus of Nazareth, the whole idea of the Cross was associated with something that man in his better moments tried to forget. It needed a miracle to change a hangman's rope into a symbol of God Himself. Men need the mountain to stretch their eyesight and uplift their gaze, but it took Jesus to change the ignoble hillock of Golgotha, littered with dead men's skulls, into Calvary, where the Mystic Cross towers over the wrecks of time.

There are many hills of man's spirit to which we may look when we are weary and disillusioned—the Acropolis, where the grace and poetry of the Parthenon laughs down the Aegean wind; there are the rough, red crags of Sinai, where the moral law rings like a trumpet to the conscience of man. But when the soul is sick we remember that Sinai was no place for sinners. Calvary has no place for anybody else. There we can take our burden and never bring it away. There is an immortal passage in the Pilgrim's Progress: "Now I saw in my dream that Christian ran till he came to a place somewhat ascending, and upon that place stood a Cross, and a little below, in the bottom, a sepulchre. So I saw in my dream that, just as Christian came up with the Cross, his burden loosed from his shoulders, and from off his back, and began to tumble till it came to the mouth of the sepulchre, where it fell in, and I saw it no more."

Every evening in Jerusalem a man used to come out on the roof of the Greek Cathedral, called the "Centre of the World." He carried a candle in his hand to light up the great Cross for the night. Whenever the Crucifixion took place, it was surely in the open air, and so the Cross that stood on Calvary has become "the Light of the World."

26

Tragedy and the Crucifixion

THERE IS NOTHING IRREVERENT in the attempt to contemplate the blackest and most glorious death in the history of mankind in the light of tragic drama.

We are living in a time which brings a sense of universal seriousness to those who as a rule like to contemplate the brighter side of life.

Men, even if they prefer comedy, have recognized the fact that the greatest literature in the world is tragic. The first classical examples came down to us from the golden days of ancient Greece. It was then that thinkers gathered in the open theatre of Athens to watch the first moving pictures of the ways of God with mankind. The English mind associates tragedy with the great plays of Shakespeare, who had an almost god-like clairvoyance about the human heart.

> *The poem hangs on the berry bush,*
> *Till comes the Poet's eye,*
> *And the whole world is a masquerade*
> *When Shakespeare passes by.*

It is a difficult matter to define tragedy. It is not enough to say that it is a story with a sad ending, or that it is a contest between good and evil. There are other elements to which we shall refer presently, but this much may be said: there are two noble interpretations in life, one is tragedy and the other is the Cross of Christ. It is a strange but true thing that preaching on the mystery suggested by these two words will touch the heart of rich and poor, wise and simple, as nothing else can.

Sometimes tragedy is the conflict of one form of good with another. Let us take the Gospel story. From the point of view of the unbiased spectator, the enemies of Jesus were quite respectable. The Pharisees represented something both great and good. Their ancestors fought bravely for freedom; they were the trustees of the law of God. It is true they were conservative, which is not always a crime. That is the way in which evil works in this world. It always assumes the plausible picture of decency before it becomes dangerous.

In ancient story the great moralists were obsessed by the words "destiny" and "fate." At the end of all their drama the spectator who saw them, and the reader of today, is filled with an overwhelming sense not only of the mystery, but of the uselessness of life. What is the use? If there is Anybody in the sky, He doesn't care. "Life is a tale told by an idiot, full of sound and fury, signifying nothing." Christianity has always denied this. The pagan hero speaks the lines and performs the acts which fate dictates to him. His struggle is in vain before he begins.

The story of Jesus on His way to Calvary is a tragedy of a unique kind. Fate is left out and God is inserted in its place. Christ is always the master and not the slave of circumstances. There is nothing more clear in the story of the final act of the Passion than that Jesus knew the consequences of every action and that His eyes were open. Even in Gethsemane He knew that the choice was His.

82

He told His disciples: "I have power to lay down my life and take it up again." This is the reason why the narrative of Good Friday stands above everything that has been written. The Evangelists, simple men as they were, rose to the nobility of their theme. There is no attempt to play on the emotions; there are no superlatives, but the simple tale that ends when the Man who saved others but could not save Himself is laid in a tomb.

Calvary was not fated, but embraced by the free choice of the Saviour of the world. The Cross is as much the defeat of fatalism as it is the defeat of sin. There is another unique quality in the Crucifixion. The Devil is not visibly destroyed within the action of the drama. Envy, hatred, cruelty and bigotry have their way with Jesus as the Gestapo have their way in the conquered lands of Europe, and yet we feel that evil was doomed from the moment when Jesus prayed for His murderers as they were nailing Him to the Cross. When Easter Day came all the villians of the piece had slept in their beds, but, somehow, you feel that their stature is growing smaller, like the scene of Alice in Wonderland. The Resurrection and the Ascension are bound up with Good Friday, and they are so great that we forget the men who thought they could conquer Christ.

27

"The Son of Man"

IT IS A DIFFICULT THING to write about the personality of
the greatest and best beloved figure who ever walked
upon this earth. Our sense of reverence bids us beware of
undue familiarity, and religious feeling has prompted
men to picture the Son of Man in stained-glass windows
and paintings which vainly try to suggest that He was
more than man. The hymns of Christendom have been
a delight and comfort to millions of hearts, but every poet
has not the genius of St. Bernard, and the fact remains
that outside of the pages of the Gospels, with their matchless simplicity, every man must see his own picture of
Jesus of Nazareth.

It is impossible for man to depict God by word, chisel
or brush, although many great men have tried. The
result has been that some have come to think that the
beautiful character of Our Lord is out of place in this
world, now so full of strife.

Is it true that the Jesus of history no longer appeals to
men? Is Christianity an abnormal dream? Let us look
for a moment at the candid camera of four very different
men as they give us a close view of Him under various
conditions over a period of three years. This is only the
human figure without a halo.

84

Jesus was young and endowed with a strong body. He was never sick. He was a carpenter by trade. He was hardy enough to sleep anywhere without luxury. But we know that sometimes He was tired. He did not hesitate to ask for a drink of cold water on a hot day.

Like all strong men, He had the gift of silence. There was always a mystery about Him. His companions and closest friends never quite understood Him. His was the loneliness of greatness.

There was a strange majesty about Him. He bore no badge of office, yet He was obeyed. He was sometimes opposed by crowds, but in personal touch with any individual He easily prevailed. Whenever He did speak, His words were like electricity.

He was never afraid. Many a time He was in a tight place. Others were frightened. Pilate feared Caesar. The rulers feared the mob. His disciples were terrified, and with a good cause, but He was calm.

Near the end it was obvious that death was waiting for him. He might have taken His friends away to a safe haven in the hills, but He set His jaw to go to the one place in Palestine where the unholy alliance of Church and State were waiting with their time bomb—yes, He was brave.

He was a genial person. He had a subtle fascination for others. Unlike many moralists, He was easy to live with. He never posed. Very common people liked to meet Him. He hated shams, both men and things. The only time He was angry was when He rebuked pompous and cynical hypocrites.

Perhaps the most outstanding impression on His contemporaries was made by His passionate pity for the sick, the poor, the brokenhearted, and the hopeless. They never forgot Him.

Finally, He saw life with clear eyes. He never promised that those who followed Him would be safe, or rich, or famous, but He did promise them happiness. He said to them what He is saying to us (if we would listen):

> If any man will come after Me let him take up his Cross and follow Me.

> > *... Do not but keep me, hope or none,*
> > *Cheery and staunch till all is done,*
> > *And at the last gasp quickly to lend*
> > *One effort more to save a friend.*
> >
> > *And when—for so I sometimes dream—*
> > *I've crossed the dark and silent stream,*
> > *Then clear, unburdened, careless, cool,*
> > *I'll saunter up from the grim pool*
> > *And join my friends; then you'll come by,*
> > *The Captain of our company,*
> > *Call me out, look me up and down,*
> > *And pass me through without a frown.*
> > *With a half smile and never a word,*
> > *And so—I shall have met my Lord!*

28

The Voice of the Wounded

THE EIGHTH OF AUGUST, 1918, was one of the great days in Canadian history. The Battle of Amiens began at twenty minutes past four in the morning. As the sun rose over Villers-Bretonneux the roads were crowded with advancing transports and returning wounded. Like the five fingers of a hand the paths led to the wrist at the great white chateau a mile from the city. By noon thousands of wounded were lying on stretchers, waiting their turn to be carried inside for surgical attention. It was very hot. From every side rose the cry, "Water, water." For several hours every available chaplain and batman was loaded down with water-bottles. Every wounded man cried, "I thirst." It was the natural cry of the wounded soldier.

So with Christ. While He was fighting with the forces of hell on the Cross and winning the salvation of man He had no time to feel His physical pain and suffering. It was only when the storm had passed that He spoke for the first and only time of His suffering and cried, "I thirst."

The greatness of our Lord's nature was never more divinely revealed than in these words, for here is an appeal of human weakness. It is only the truly great who can forgive with that last generosity of forgiveness which begs for help from those who have done the wrong.

St. John is the only Gospel-writer who preserves this fifth word from the Cross, probably because, at the end of the first century, there were those who denied the true humanity of Jesus.

His thirst was the result of His physical and mental sufferings. He was thirsty in body, soul and spirit. His passion was borne in the perfection of His human nature.

There are three draughts mentioned in the Crucifixion story:

First, the proffered opiate provided by the charitable ladies of Jerusalem to stupefy the tortured criminal. Jesus refused it.

The second is the mock wassail cup—the caricature of coronation wine pledged in mockery by the soldiers.

The third He accepted—sour soldiers' wine, soaked in a sponge, given by a soldier who had some pity in his heart.

But this cry of the dying Christ suggests another thirst, His thirst for souls.

Once in His ministry the Saviour rested by the well at Samaria. To the woman who gave Him water He spoke of the "Living water." And now, again "wearied with His journey," about the sixth hour, He is purchasing for all men the living water. This is the mystical significance of the only cry of pain that Jesus ever uttered. The Gospels do not encourage that type of piety which glories in the physical sufferings of Calvary. Yet we must be grateful for this one word, for it reminds us that the Saviour of the world was truly human. He shared our life of instinct and desire. He felt the pull and repulsion of pleasure and of pain. It is strange that our Lord should have allowed one who had perhaps helped to nail Him

88

to the Cross to provide the one touch of kindness in all this scene of cruelty. We still have our chance to give something to One who needs nothing now.

In that picture of the Last Judgment those who are welcomed are only those who have done those "little nameless, unremembered acts of kindness and of love." "Come ye blessed of My Father." "For I was thirsty and ye gave me drink." It is not possible! When? How? Where?

"Inasmuch as we have done it unto one of the least of these My brethren, ye have done it unto Me." Wherever the old and sick are suffering in lonely rooms, wherever there is a wet pillow in a public ward in the hospital, there Christ is saying, "I thirst." The cry of Jesus is the wail of the slums, of the friendless, the curse of the ticket-of-leave man with furtive eyes looking for a job.

How He must rejoice to see some one step out of the crowd, even though it seems foolish, in answer to the Divine pathos in the cry of this suffering world.

29

The Voice of a Son

AT THE FOOT OF THE CROSS, through the hours of the Crucifixion, stood a group of friends, and among them there were two who have caught the imagination of the Christian world. In the pictures of the Crucifixion, with true insight, the Mother of Jesus is generally represented on one side of the Cross and St. John on the other. These two are chosen because the Saviour loved them best.

It is significant that of all the friends and followers of our Lord it was the women who were chiefly represented at Calvary. There is something very human in that picture, because women remain by the bed of pain and men have the instinct to slip away. Peter and his companions were scattered; most likely they were in hiding. It has always been the way of mothers to stand by their sons when others have deserted them.

> "If I were damned of body and soul,
>   I know whose prayers would make me whole—
> Mother o' Mine."

There are three relationships which Christ maintained in His earthly life: His Divine relation to God, His redemptive link with mankind, and His human relation to His mother. It is a great mistake for Christians to lose sight of this fact, for in it are to be found beautiful lights on the character of Christ. It is a wonderful consolation to us that, when the Son of God became man, He entered into the world through the lowly gate of human birth and that He lived as a child in Nazareth. His first memories were in a little village among the humblest of His nation.

Let us meditate for a moment on the position of Mary as she stood before the Cross. Many thoughts must have come to her mind: The scene in the Temple long years before when Simeon had said to her, "A sword shall pierce through thy own soul also"; the vision of the Annunciation; the angels' song over the fields of Bethlehem that night when her Son was born. What hopes she had! What dreams for Him as the story of His early Galilean ministry reached the little cottage in Nazareth; and later, when the gathering storm began to break, she is a picture of the tragedy and glory of all mothers who send out their sons into the rough, cruel world and pray for them. "For men must work and women must weep"—it is a universal song of humanity.

There is a depth of meaning in these words as the dying Saviour looks on His mother and whispers, "Woman, behold thy Son"—and yet there is something that He can give to His mother. "Stripped of everything," said Godet, "Jesus seemed to have nothing more to give." Nevertheless He had already made precious gifts. He had prayed for His murderers; He had given pardon to His companion on the Cross; and now He leaves the last and greatest legacy of love to those two whom He loved most when He bound their broken lives together by a word to each.

"Woman, behold thy son." There is not the least disrespect or coldness in this greeting, which seems rather cruel to English ears. The word "gunai," which is the same that was used when Jesus spoke to His mother on the occasion of the miracle in Cana of Galilee, is the same that King Agamemnon used to his Queen. It is a title of honor and also is significant of Mary's prophetic relationship to the great event of Calvary. It was the seed of the woman that should bruise the serpent's head.

It was a great compliment to John's character that Jesus should have given him the honor of caring for His Mother, and so in the words "Son, behold thy mother" there is an eternal message to every young man to reverence motherhood above all earthly titles.

We learn from this last word consideration for others. Suffering is proverbially selfish. The sufferer very often thinks only of himself. When was ever pain so considerate as on the Cross?

Again, in this message from the Cross we learn Christ's reverence for womanhood. It is only stating truth to say that Christ's gift to woman was one of the most glorious bequests in human history; and the women of the Christian Church, with instinctive understanding and love, have sensed that in this world, which is often called a man's world, Jesus Christ has been their greatest defender. There is also in these words a benediction of the home life. Human society is founded on the family, and the Christian family takes its root from the Cross. Nations rise and fall as they value the spiritual quality of family life. History teaches us that when the family begins to go, the glory of the nation is near its end.

Finally, there seems to be a suggestion here that the Church of Christ should not be a lonely place. It has been a solace for countless myriads through the ages, but in our modern city life it would sometimes appear that the sad and lonely are overlooked in the family life of organized religion. Surely the old and the bereaved should find comfort in the Church.

30

'When It Was Dark'

DARKNESS OF NIGHT: Not a light in the house of Caiaphas, not a light in the house of Pilate. All is now silence and darkness where the torches flared, and the fire burned in the middle of the court, where soldiers stood on duty, and messengers were moving to and fro, and the Council of the Sanhedrin was in session. Only in the temple a dim lamp burns before the torn veil of the Holy Place; and in the sky the paschal moon is shining, casting black shadows beneath the olive trees of Gethsemane, and showing the crosses of Calvary in dim outline. The whole world lies in darkness.

Darkness of despair: Jesus of Nazareth, whom some had called the Christ, is dead. His life had ended as all clearsighted persons had long seen that it must end. There was a time when enthusiastic crowds gathered about Him, and when there seemed to be so many who believed in Him that some impulsive disciples proposed to make Him the leader of a Messianic revolution, and went so far as to proclaim Him their King. But He had promptly and decisively discouraged them, and had, as it seemed, even wantonly, disappointed all His followers; He had contradicted all ambition; He had disregarded all the arts of popularity. He had chosen His friends from among peasants, fishermen and publicans, all of them poor and obscure, some of them markedly disapproved by good people. He had opposed Himself to those who had political and ecclesiastical authority. He had made it plain as day that if He came into possession of powers He would turn out all mercenary politicians and expel all irreligious priests. Naturally, they hated Him. Day by day they persuaded the people against Him. And the crucifixion had been the logical end of the matter. It had put a seal of condemnation upon a course of failure.

Darkness of sin: Wickedness has triumphed. The one strong Man in all the nation who had dared to stand out against the iniquities of the time is dead. Jesus of Nazareth is dead; by irreligious priests and mercenary politicians, seized and killed. These men represented the condition of both Church and State.

Religion was devoted to the upbuilding of an ecclesiastical establishment. Its emphasis was set on ritual; it cared less for righteousness. Its concern was for externals. It had ceased to uplift the daily life of man, ceased to make men brotherly, ceased to make men better. It had become a foolish thing of ceremonies and attitudes and gorgeous garments and hindering traditions.

Darkness of sorrow: A graveyard and a company of mourners. A familiar sight. Every day men and women with tears in their eyes are going out in procession to new graves. Jesus Christ has met the fate of human kind! What is death? It is the beginning of new life, we avow. The soul, freed from its hindering limitations, goes on into another country, into another kind of living, better and richer. The souls of the faithful, after they are delivered from the burden of the flesh, are in joy and felicity. How do we know?

How do we know that the soul lives? Love, indeed,

94

whispered it, and hope whispered it, to the soul of man; but knowledge kept still silence. Oh, that the black wall might open, that the blank and awful barrier might have a door in it! Oh, that some one who had died might come back to tell us! But on went the unending procession of mourners, and nobody came back. What lay beyond the grave no philosopher, no saint, could tell. The life of the world to come was but an eager guess. It was yet dark.

And then the light began to shine: Mary comes again to the tomb. She sits by the door of the sepulchre, dreary and weeping. And there is a sound beside her, and One stands in the faint radiance of the increasing dawn, and a voice, well known and tender, speaks her name. At last we know. Jesus Christ has come back out of the grave to tell us. He who was dead, behold, He lives, and is alive, evermore, and has the keys of death and of the grave.

31

Recognition In Eternity

EASTER, THE GREAT CHRISTIAN FESTIVAL, touches the primal instinct of humanity. The hope of immortality is the foundation of all religion. It is no mere figure of speech to say that Christianity is built on an empty tomb.

The Festival of the Resurrection reminds man that he is more than a child of time. The glory and the poetry of the teaching of this day are to be found in the spirit of the service. Christmas and Easter are the two days when music and flowers express more than sober prose.

Among all the thoughts which come unbidden to our hearts there is none more universal and more human than the thought of recognition in heaven. Most of us are glad to think that our personality shall live beyond the grave, but if we were concerned only with our own future we can well imagine that many a Christian might almost be reconciled to Nirvana after the fitful fever of life. We might think that life was hardly worth while if it were to end in oblivion; that God was less than kind to have created such a poignant experiment as life and then throw away the once-used die; but, nevertheless, we say for ourselves that we could be reconciled to an everlasting sleep.

But when we think of those we love it is very different. In this world of death a message of reunion in eternity is a first necessity. It is as music to all souls in pain. We do not say that it is always listened to by the bereaved in the first force of passionate misery while they feel in their breasts the burning of the murderous steel, but there comes through faith at length the calm and acknowledged loss settling deep and still over the subduing days of life. After that may come the peace of believing and the hope of Easter Day.

This hope concerns only those who believe in Christ. Apart from His being, His dying, His rising again, and His testimony, there is no doctrine of the future. The essence of personal Christianity lies in love to a personal Saviour. He has abolished death by His resurrection. He has risen and ascended and He rules. In His safe-keeping are all faithful souls and we may surely say the bodies which were once the robes and the homes of these spirits.

It is He who takes care of the passing soul, and as a magnet draws it upward to Himself. Because He is the Centre, as we draw nigh to Him we feel that we are drawing nearer to our loved ones who have gone before. He, who inspired human love that now seeks its own, will never deny our heart's desire.

It may be said that this excludes the vast majority, but it is not so. We do not know what may pass in the very moment of dying between the soul and Christ. All the great Christian teachers have told us that the very slightest recognition of the Divine Sacrifice is enough to secure salvation.

In his two sermons on "The Penitent Thief," Charles Spurgeon refuses to admit that he is dealing with a solitary case. He says that if the thief was an exceptional thief there would have been a hint given of so important a fact. Would not the Saviour have whispered quietly to the dying man, "You are the only one I am going to treat this way"? No, our Lord spoke openly. Moreover, the inspired penman has recorded it. If it had been an exceptional case it would not have been written in the Word of God.

Reunion rests upon the permanence of personality. Through all the changes of mind and body something remains which we call "I," and that individual life will pass through courses which the sun dare not enter, survive all kinds of temporal and spiritual wreck, move uninjured through fallen worlds, meet undismayed the ghosts of the whole earth, pass undestroyed through the joys of angels, perhaps also through anguish which would dissolve the stars. It is true that we shall, in the next life, find more to know and more to love than has been our lot on earth.

I shall find them again, I shall find them again,
  By the soul that within me dwells,
And leaps unto Thee with rapture free,
  As the jubilant anthem swells.

"I heard a voice saying." What it says,
  I hear. So perchance do they,
As I stand between my living, I ween,
  And my dead, on Easter Day.

32

"A-wearying for Christ"

THE GREAT EASTER FESTIVAL is over. The sun seemed to shine with difficulty this year. It seemed as if Nature herself had been influenced by the tragedy of the world. Now that the music is fading in the distance, there are many whose hearts were lifted for a time by the Resurrection story who ask themselves: "Was it all a dream? Where is the Risen Christ?"

The same question was asked nearly two thousand years ago. The question did not come from Jerusalem, but on the shores of a little lake a hundred miles away. Seven of the men who saw the vision in the Upper Room were lured by some homing instinct to the place where they first saw their Lord. Galilee is not much larger than Lake Muskoka—64 square miles, with deep bays, and water of an incredible blue. It is a miracle in the deepest canyon in the world just below the level of the sea. If they had to wait, they felt that they would rather spend the time in familiar surroundings than in the hard, cruel streets of the great city.

Our modern world has much the same feeling. There are sorrowful hearts who would like to be assured that the great Friend of mankind still lives and that it is possible to hear His voice. The Gospel still reminds us that there are times when God seems lost when we need

99

Him most. The idyll of the lake also tells us that what we long for is often nearer than we think. We should remember also that the thought which hearts us to face the inevitable changes also gives dignity, beauty and poetry to the small, prosaic present. "Jesus Christ is the same today." We are always tempted to think that this moment is commonplace and insignificant. Yesterday lies consecrated in memory, tomorrow radiant in hope, but our war-torn today is poverty-stricken and prose. The sky is furthest away from us right over our heads. Behind and in front it seems to touch the earth. But if we will only realize that all that sparkling lustre and that immortal tenderness of pity and of love with which religion has irradiated and sweetened some sacred hour is here with us amid the dusty duties of today, then we need not look back to any purple horizon or forward to what may be a mirage, but be sure that here or nowhere is Christ, the unchanging Friend.

There seems to be a lesson from the Christian Church —after such an Eastertide as that which came this year. There was always a touch of genius in Simon Peter. He was the one who said, "I go a-fishing." It was the best thing that he could have suggested. Izaak Walton was right in his estimate of the value of the most ancient of all human recreations. The first disciples were commissioned by their master to be fishers of men.

The modern Church is busy—perhaps too busy—but it has always used traditional methods. We are living under strange conditions, but we still cling to the conventional tackle—preaching, ritual, music and dignity. What about the nets . . . ? We still seem to hear the voice on that April morning when tired and discouraged laborers were startled by the words, "Cast on the right side of the boat, and ye shall find." It is impossible for any Christian not to ask himself: "Is the Church saving souls? Is it helping men and women to be better?" If not, let the dead bury their dead.

As we look to the boat on that little lake early in the morning, we feel that we are gazing upon a microcosm of the world. They feel lonely and deserted, just as the Christian Church in many of the persecuted countries of Europe seems today. Christ had withdrawn. He was not to be seen, yet He was watching them all the time. They were never more precious than in that dark, discouraging night. As a matter of fact, the future of the world was in that boat.

There was an old revival hymn which began, "I feel like singing all the time." Unfortunately there are times when we could not sing if we tried, but it is in moments like that that duty still remains. Peter was no scholar, but there were some things that he could do. When the heart is heavy, when talk of trust in God seems idle chatter . . . "I go a-fishing." There is still work to be done. It is hard to take up the cross, even in the sunshine, but it leads to a peace more exquisite than music, to a trust in God that blossoms red, though its roots are in the silent grave.

33

Under One Roof

THE CHAPTER WHICH CONTAINS the noblest prose in the English language begins with the words, "Comfort ye, comfort ye, my people, saith your God." We cannot doubt that there is a place for the Gospel of Comfort in the cycle of religious teaching. Let it never be forgotten that this is not the beginning of religion. The first words of the Bible remind us that God is above all; in Him we live and move and have our being. He was before us; He is all around us; we are part of Him. The categorical imperative of conscience proves to us that He is the everlasting Judge. In His own time and in His own way He punishes evil in men and nations, and rewards purity, faithfulness and truth. It should not be forgotten that He is King. In a memorable passage in the Book of the Revelation, which somehow suggests the spirit of this very hour when the earth is cracking, when the seas are roaring and lightning terrifies, suddenly, like an anthem with organ accompaniment, come the words, "Halleluia, the Lord Omnipotent reigneth."

If this were the whole of religion, life would be too exalted and impersonal for the average human soul. Christianity shows us that the face of God is friendly, and that He who has placed us in a world where much of our happiness depends on others lays no burden upon us greater than we can bear. Our hopes and fears, our sorrows and our joys are known to Him, who is Father as well as God. Let us think for a moment about the personal comfort of religion.

We are living in a time when our hearts and minds are lifted to the plane of sacrifice by such words as truth, freedom and patriotism, but each one of us has a life to live with himself, and it is here that the Gospel of Comfort brings a medicine prescribed by the Great Physician. The greatest tragedy on this planet at the present time is not the sinking of huge ships that have cost millions of dollars, nor the blasting of the Dnieper Dam or the destruction of beautiful buildings; it is the loss of men who are loved by some one watching at home. It was a profound theologian who said that wherever men fall they fall into the arms of infinite love. The biggest and most precious verses of Holy Scripture are those which give that assurance.

> *I know not where His islands lift*
> *Their fronded palms in air,*
> *I only know I cannot drift*
> *Beyond His love and care.*

Perhaps it is wise not to think too much about Hong Kong, Singapore and Coventry in terms of human grief. An American poet has said that our saddest thought of the dead is the fear of their unovertakableness. They have gone before, and we cannot overtake them. Who has not at one time or another been oppressed by that feeling? They are out of our reach, past our touch, and their new country is a land that is very far off.

As the Easter festival draws near we think of the Sabbath when Jesus lay all alone in the rock-hewn sepulchre, and yet He was one Traveller who did return. It is not a romancer but an eyewitness who says: "Let not your heart be troubled: ye believe in God, believe also in me. In my Father's house are many mansions." It is a comfort to think that when we die we can overtake our loved ones at once, and hold them for our very own. This hope is rooted in Christ, who died and rose again. He gave the love on both sides, and that love is immortal even when the outward tokens of it are more or less withdrawn. Therefore, even now we can joyfully explain, in spite of time, death and change, we are still all together. It is a woman's heaven to have all she loves beneath one roof.

> *So I can go up to bed,*
>   *Pass the doors where once I heard*
> *Gentle breathing, as I crept*
>   *Softly by, without a word:*
> *Though the house is silent now,*
>   *Though they wish me no good-night—*
> *We are still beneath one roof—*
>   *When I bar the door at night.*

34

The Miracle of Spring

MODERN MAN HAS MADE so many little miracles of his own that he has almost come to think that he needs no help from his Creator. In his long struggle against the rigors of nature he has paid for his comfort by missing some of the most thrilling surprises of God. The sunrise and the sunset, the fleecy clouds drifting in a blue sky, and daily pictures from the brush of the great Artist who knows that man needs something to kindle his imagination and stir his deep capacity for spiritual rapture.

God made summer and winter, but His masterpiece of painting is Spring.

With our central heating, air-conditioned houses, refrigeration and rapid transport, we not only live in a summer climate in the winter at home, but our cars are warm in January. The old strawberry festival has lost its thrill to those who can pick summer fruits and flowers on Yonge Street, while their ancestors were sleeping with a hot brick and eating salt pork and dried apples.

Do we ever think how people in the North passionately long for the miracle of the coming sun? Years ago at Albany on Hudson Bay in this very week an unusually long winter was coming to an end. The old Hudson's Bay Company fort stood on the banks of the river as it had done for more than two centuries. The Indians were hungry and tired. The rabbits had failed and provisions were low. The people looked drawn and sad. Several had died. There was a funeral in the white log church whose shining tin spire was glittering with the first warm days of the year. There was still snow on the ground; the ice was three feet thick in the river, but it was black and rotten—no one could cross. The Burial Service in the church was over and the men in their capotes carried the rough wooden coffin while the women, with their black shawls held tight over their heads, made a cavalcade of woe. The Missionary walked in front, treading warily among the tents where husky dogs prowled, on his way to the little graveyard where two men with pickaxes had been for hours chipping the frozen earth deep enough to make a shallow trench. Although in the morning the whole scene looked and felt like the ragged end of winter, now the South wind grows warmer every moment and already the haze is seen in quivering waves over the melting ice and snow.

As the cortege was lost in the maze of wigwams, suddenly the cry of wild geese was heard. The funeral procession stood still and from all over the settlement came the answering call from every living soul. A great flock of Canada grey geese swept like a gigantic airplane over the trees rejoicing at what seemed a welcoming call. The phalanx turned to leeward and sailed slowly down over the spot from which the sounds came. It was too much even for sorrow and decorum. The Chief Mourner dived into his tent and appeared in a moment with his loaded gun. With incredible ease and grace he brought down a goose with each barrel. Cheers and laughter rang out. The oldest instinct of man triumphed in every simple heart and as the pallbearers patted the bereaved husband on the back he modestly replied like a true sportsman, "She did it. I always had luck when she was with me." Then the spell was broken; the procession resumed its direction.

Only those who have lived through a Northern winter can understand that story. The wild goose is the harbinger of Spring. His coming means warmth, friendly sunlight, food and health. It is an assurance that all's well with the world and that "Kitche Munetoo" has not forgotten his children. That is the secret of the exultant cry from the river bank.

Every one who has smelled the pungent smoke of burning weeds in an early Spring garden knows that the gardener is a priest. Lord Bacon's words are true, "Gardening is the purest of human pleasures and the greatest refreshment to the spirit of man." The Spring of our human story blossomed in a garden. The gardens of Ontario will soon be aflame. There is surely medicine there for anxious and weary spirit. Always the shrubs are awake. There is Religion as well as infinite philosophy in the lines of Florence Mastin entitled "Forsythia" in the New York Times:

> *When the spring rain was saying, "Hush,"*
> *Lo, on the hill, the burning bush!*
>
> *Among grey leaves it flamed alone*
> *As though God's breath had on it blown.*
>
> *Its frosty boughs dripped golden light*
> *As though His touch had made them bright.*
>
> *And from its heart a hidden bird*
> *Spoke suddenly His secret word.*

35

Summer and Winter

OUR CANADIAN SUMMER comes with a rush that is overwhelming. Over three million square miles of our country the transformation of a few weeks is almost incredible. The people of the Northern Zone appreciate their summer because, in the background of their minds, there is the memory of winter.

Poets and preachers have often spoken of the spiritual lessons of the summer, but it is seldom that any poet is inspired to sing the mournful numbers of a February blizzard.

From one point of view summer and winter are but other names for optimism and pessimism, which are part of the furniture of human existence. Every man and woman knows the meaning of the summer and winter of spiritual experiences in the individual life of the universe of the soul.

In the story of nations recorded in history there are years and decades of alternating darkness and light. There are seasons, alas too regular, of growth, meridian and the falling of autumn leaves, followed by winter, which sometimes brings no spring.

In the story of the world the same spiritual truth can easily be traced. There have been periods in human history when men have dreamed dreams and their hands have stretched to the stars. Those have been the bright, warm summer days of the human race, always followed by the twilight and darkness of pessimism. In days like our own, when man has come down from the mountain peaks to the valley of depression, the Christian is cheered by the magnificent optimism of Christ. He looked steadily at the terrible evil of the world without once feeling despair. Believing in men, He recreated them; believing in life, He revolutionized it.

Mary's song in the Magnificat is gloriously triumphant. She sings of the wickedness of the proud and the sufferings of the hungry, but she also tells of God who scatters the one and cares for the other. That must be our faith in Christian Canada today. We expect pessimism from the materialists, but it is unpardonable in Christians. Surely it is one of the great duties of the Church of Jesus Christ to pierce the veil of disappointment and depression which shrouds our modern life, to force men to see the radiant vision of its glorious possibilities, to stir and stimulate mankind by awakening men's faith in their capacity of great achievement, to put to its lips as it stands in the trenches the golden trumpet of the victorious Christ and to sound a reveille of hope.

Winter will not last forever; summer will come again.

> *"Say not the struggle naught availeth,*
> *The labor and the wounds are vain,*
> *The enemy faints not nor faileth,*
> *And as things have been they remain.*
>
> *"For while the tired waves vainly breaking*
> *Seem here no painful inch to gain,*
> *Far back, through creeks and inlets making,*
> *Comes silent, flooding-in, the main."*

36

"The Glorious Company"

WHITSUNDAY IS THE BIRTHDAY of the Christian Church. However mystical your religion may be, you are transported from the Holy of Holies into the Main Street of human life.

In the words of the second chapter of the Acts of the Apostles there is a suggestion of a world's fair. We have a picture of many nations in the list of Peter's first congregation. You can hear the short, incisive speech of the Roman, the musical cadences of the Greek tongue, the guttural of the Arab, and you can see the rainbow-colored robes of the East and the red cloaks of the Imperial legions, and the white togas of the scholars brought before your eyes.

In that scene in the streets of Jerusalem there is a picture of all the ages. We are witnessing the birth of the Christian Church.

We generally think of the twelve Apostles rather vaguely and impersonally as a group of saintly men, with haloes around their heads, but to those who knew them they were much like ourselves. One of the most original things that Jesus ever did was His selection of the men who were to build the Christian Church. They were not university graduates, they were not the great men of the nation. They were a group largely of hard-fisted fishermen who spoke the patois of Galilee. And yet there is something very suggestive in the list of the twelve Apostles, which we find in four different places in the New Testament.

As we look at the names we see that there are three groups.

First, there are the men of genius. Peter is always at the top—the great, impetuous, warm-hearted disciple, who loved his Lord in spite of his denial. Then Andrew, his brother, and James and John—Andrew, the practical man who worked for Christ; John, the mystic and the poet; James the Son of Thunder, who died when he was still young. These were the leaders of the Apostles.

The second group of the Apostles are the average men. Philip and Nathanael, Matthew and Thomas. They loved Jesus too, but they are smaller men—useful, practical. It took some of them a long time to believe in Christ. They could not help it; they were made that way.

Look at Philip. One day Jesus asked him, "Whence shall we buy bread that these may eat?" But Philip did not rise to the test. He begins to calculate the price in a baker's shop. He said it would take $200 worth of bread (that was the value in our own money).

Nathanael was different. He was a canny man. He had his doubts about any good thing coming out of Nazareth, but the moment he met Jesus his doubt was over—an honest, pure-minded man, straight as a string. "Behold, an Israelite indeed in whom there is no guile."

We always think of Thomas as a doubter. Did you ever know a man or a woman who always saw the dark side of things? That was Thomas. Yet, you remember, in spite of that, he was willing to die with Christ, and his confession in the twilight of that upper room has thrilled the Church for two thousand years.

Matthew was the business man, and a shady business at that. He was a tax-gatherer, and the Roman method of farming out the taxes was something like the Chinese—every little tax-gatherer got his squeeze. No wonder the Jews hated them. Picture the scene when Jesus first passed by his office in Capernaum and saw him selling out a poor fisherman who was behind in his taxes.

The last group are the obscure. We only know their names and, strange to say, they seem to have been very strict, religious men. Simon, the zealot, and James, later the first Bishop of Jerusalem; and Judas, the man of affairs, who looked after the business end of the mission. There was another Judas of whom we know nothing except that he once asked a rather stupid question.

May we not take these twelve men as representing the material to be found in any Christian Church? Jesus wants and calls all sorts of people—the genius, the enthusiast, the blunderer, the doubter, the ignorant and stupid. He wants us all. He wants among the clergy those leaders in the Old Land like Gore and Inge and Hensley Henson and Studdert-Kennedy, the prophets of God. He needs, too, the poor, awkward parson without much genius or eloquence, whose loving life is a continual sermon.

Remember that the twelve Apostles, according to the view of their own Church, were only twelve laymen. Jesus wants the glad, confident Christian with vision and the power of organization. He wants the man with money to dedicate himself to the greatest of all causes. He needs the genial, kindly man who makes religion attractive, and the silent, reserved man.

112

The tragedy of Christianity is that men and Churches of diverse types never understand or appreciate each other. One does not need to go back to the Middle Ages or the Reformation to illustrate this. John Strachan and Egerton Ryerson each made a contribution to the religious history of Ontario.

37

The Plain Man and the Trinity

OUR EARLIEST RECOLLECTIONS of Trinity Sunday were always associated with that strange document called the Athanasian Creed. We always looked with intense interest for the rolling thunder of the damnatory clauses "which faith except a man keep whole and undefiled, without doubt he will perish everlastingly." For years the moral sense of many people was shocked by the tone of this venerable document. It was to be said or sung on all the festivals, and it was appropriately associated with the service on Trinity Sunday. Many a stout layman had folded his arms and stiffened his jaw and glared at the meek parson as he recited this confession of faith of the gentle Christ.

At a meeting of the General Synod of the Church of England when the Prayer Book was being revised, the laity were unanimously against the compulsory recitation of the Athanasian Creed. One distinguished Bishop seriously suggested that the sentences should be so arranged that the offending clauses should be recited only by the clergy.

One needs vision to understand historical matters. We should remember that this Creed comes to us over a bridge of 1,500 years. It was formulated at the end of a terrible controversy which shook the Christian Church to its foundations. Kings and monks and martyrs prayed and fought with the passionate conviction that the dignity of our Saviour was at stake. Our personal belief is that, if the apparently innocent Arian heresy had won, Christianity would have died centuries ago.

It is a strange commentary on human nature that we always marvel at the passionate excitement of great movements in other ages, forgetting that some placid historian may have precisely the same opinion of some of our own headlines today. We also can be very dogmatic about slogans and watchwords the meaning of which is not clear to ourselves. Probably the great Creed of Trinity Sunday was intended to be sung. You can see the eyes of the Bishops blazing with mingled divine and human triumph as they rolled the periods which tried to define a mystery which transcends the mind of man.

Trinity Sunday is not a war dance over heretics; it commemorates a very real thing. It is our witness that human life is not spanned by the narrow horizon of the obvious. It is a confession that we trust in the living God who made heaven and earth, and that this God is our Saviour, and that He dwells in the hearts of men. One of the things that we need to learn is that there are some mysteries left.

The average Christian would be stumped if he were asked to give a picture of the Trinity. The stained-glass windows of our Churches have attempted to do so. There is God the Father, a venerable figure enthroned in rainbow and amethyst, with a sceptre in His hand and a far-away look in His eyes. On His right hand, the figure of Christ glorified, but still with the mark of the thorns and nails. On the left, the Dove, enshrined in a halo; somehow the Three suggesting a certain unity.

There are three elements in the doctrine of the Trinity. First, we believe in God, the Creator of the world, in Whom we live and move and have our being. Bruno, in his prison, touched a straw which lay on the floor, saying that from that straw he could prove that there was a God. The poor sailors with Franklin in the Erebus and Terror saw God amid the icebergs of the Arctic night.

But a God who sits in His heaven is no good to us. Therefore, we need Jesus, the Son of Man. Man can never complain that God is remote when we think of the story of Him who walked through the cornfields of Galilee and died upon a cross that men might have hope 2,000 years afterwards. And if any one thinks that the Holy Spirit is superfluous, he should be good enough to tell us what it is that has kept Christianity going through all the civilizations of our modern ages. We cannot rationalize this, but somehow we know that the truth is there.

Finally, the Christian is convinced that God is One. We do not know whether we are speaking heresy when we suggest that in other planets God might not reveal himself in a threefold way, but tenfold. It may be that in other parts of the universe there are beings and conditions so different from our own that the final doctrine of the Trinity would be unintelligible. There is a strange passage in the New Testament which we read at the burial service; it is full of dynamite, for it suggests something that we scarcely dare express in words. Here it is:

> And when all things shall be subdued unto Him, then shall the Son also Himself be subject unto Him that put all things under Him, that God may be all in all.

38

The Brittannic-American Brotherhood

THERE IS AN UNWRITTEN BOND between the people of the United States of America and those who live in the far-flung British Empire. It is not true that the British, or even the English, are of one blood. Their various flexible types, ideas and originality bear witness to the mingling, through their long history, of the Anglo-Saxons, the Celts, the Romans and the Normans. The same thing is more apparently true concerning Americans. Some one asked whether there was a special prayer for Americans in the old English Prayer Book and the answer was:

"You can find it in the petition for all sorts and conditions of men."

But a wise Englishman happily replied:

"That petition was made for the English, and fits them."

Speaking generally, we have the same history; we come from the same stock; we have the same heroes between the 10th and 18th centuries. Long before there was any thought of a formal alliance of the English-speaking peoples, there was a mystic tie which united them in spite of themselves and without their knowledge.

We are all influenced by our history. In that glorious eleventh chapter of the Epistle to the Hebrews you can find the honor roll of the people of Israel. It comes as a surprise to us to learn that the old prophets did not hesitate to speak to their people of the glorious deeds of their ancestors with a religious intensity. We too easily take it for granted that we must look to the Sacred Canon alone for our inspiration and comfort in these days of world destiny. If we could reincarnate the author of the Epistle to the Hebrews, he would ask us to turn our eyes to the glorious history of God's dealing for a thousand years. We can imagine the writer making such verses as these:

By faith, Alfred the Great gathered the scattered tribes of Albion in the ninth century, and laid the foundation of the English nation.

By faith, Edward the Confessor builded Westminster Abbey, to be a shrine forever in lands not yet discovered.

By faith, John Wycliffe translated the Word of God from a dead language into a living tongue.

By faith, Drake and Raleigh sailed the uncharted seas and carried the soul of England to distant parts of the world.

By faith, John Milton wrote of Paradise Lost, and when he was blind, sang of the city where they need no candle, neither light of the sun.

By faith, John Hampden resisted a tyrant king and died for liberty on Chalgrove Field.

By faith, Abraham Lincoln freed the slaves and saved the Union; hopeful in disaster, in victory he was merciful, and with charity toward all and hatred toward none he strove to bind up his nation's wounds. In dying, he joined the Immortals.

By faith, Thomas Edison searched for the gifts which God had hidden for man to find; he made the deaf to hear; he made his country a family; and to those who since the beginning of life on this planet had nightly sat in darkness he turned their night into day.

And what more shall I say, then? For the time would fail me to tell of Shakespeare, and Newton, and Jane Addams, who through faith subdued kingdoms, obtained promises, stopped the mouths of lions, and waxed valiant in fight.

Others had trial of modern warfare; they were bombed; they lived in dugouts; they were starved and tormented. Women received their dead raised to life again through the promise of the Resurrection.

* * * * *

Who shall estimate the influence of the English Bible on the two hundred millions who speak our tongue? In Lincoln Park in Chicago there is a statue to the greatest man that England ever produced. He was not a soldier, but a poet. Here is the inscription:

> *"He was not for an age, but for all time,*
> *our many-minded Shakespeare."*

Our united peoples stand for the common loyalties of the human race.

> *Laws, Freedoms, Truth and Faith in God*
> *Came with those exiles o'er the waves,*
> *And where their pilgrim feet have trod*
> *The God of Freedom guards their graves.*

The Niagara River is a parable of the story of the English-speaking people. It is the dividing line between the British Empire and America. The waters coming from the great inland seas are compressed into the swift rapids of the Niagara River—a symbol of the early difficulties and misunderstandings of the 18th century.

Then we come to the great Cataract, which stands for the revolution and the separate destiny of the two English-speaking nations. Below there is the whirlpool and the gorge of the 19th century, with alternate rapids and still water succeeding each other; and then the river emerges into Lake Ontario, and beyond that it flows through the great river of the St. Lawrence, ever wider and deeper, until it reaches the ocean.

Such is the story of our people. In the beginning there is the cataclysm and the rending of the rocks, the whirlpool, the rapids. But now, thank God, we have emerged into the smoother and broader water, and it may be that together our common destiny shall flow between the banks of the Divine purpose into the great ocean of Eternity.

39

An Empire's Bivouac

DURING THE FIRST GREAT WAR, after the glorious and tragic episode of the Dardanelles, a strange and moving poem appeared in the *Australasian Intercollegian*. It was written by a college student at Suvla Bay on the eve of a memorable battle. It is a simple picture of The Christ as the soldier's comrade:

> *Jesus whose lot with us was cast,*
> *Who saw it out from first to last,*
> *Who, when Your hour came, did not fail*
> *(The world's fate hanging in the scale)*
> *With Your own friends at eve to dine*
> *And talked across the bread and wine,*
> *Who then went out to face the end*
> *Alone without a single friend . . .*

The boy who scribbled those lines by the embers at his last bivouac goes on to say that when his ordeal is over, when the river is crossed, he expects the Captain of his soul to meet him on the bank with a nod and a smile and never a word.

The British Empire tonight, as we write these lines, keeps a more fateful vigil than even the Anzacs did under the stars across the strait from the plains of Troy.

In this solemn hour it is permitted to each one of us to make his own orisons and think of that strange supper in the upper room nearly two thousand years ago. The disciples were ordinary men even as we are. They had failed often in the past. They had been unworthy of that bright Spirit who was their leader. But now they knew that they all loved the things which He had tried to teach them. The only traitor was gone. His footsteps sounded on the stairs as he went out into the dark.

We, too, are dazed, and yet we feel that, unworthy as we are, we have been chosen to enter the mystery of sacrifice and faith in the Calvary of the ages.

When the Founder of Christianity finished His earthly career, He had trained a few friends. But the future did not depend on a committee, but on a sacrament which promised that little band security, continuity and strength to resist all dangers. Outside the bombs of hate were falling, but here within was the secret of victory. . . .

On the table were bread and wine. He took the common loaf in His hand and broke it in pieces and said, "Take and eat this, it is My body."

Bread has been the symbol of nourishment for the human body ever since man tilled the soil; the universal food, not to be stored but eaten; the secret of life.

Here is the secret of the ages for our race. God is necessary to man's life. Without the Divine Instinct man is only one of the lesser animals. Perhaps we have forgotten in our lordly progress that the true calories of the spirit are more necessary than synthetic vitamins. God has made us for Himself. Nothing else is so important as that truth.

The bread must be broken; and the Divine Essence, like the alabaster box, must be sacrificed if the being we call man is to be saved. Justice, freedom, purity, gentleness and laughter are all part of God.

122

He took the wine cup in His hands. "Drink ye all of this, for it is My blood."

In the lands of the Orient the wine was part of every little household, tended with loving care on the rocky ledges of Palestine. It was the one universal luxury. The Harvest of the Grapes was the annual festival of joy.

The wine "poured out." Then His blood must be poured out, too.

The law of sacrifice is the deepest mystery of life.

Measure thy life by loss instead of gain,
Not by the wine drunk but the wine poured forth,
For love's strength standeth in love's sacrifice
And he hath most to give who suffers most.

Heaven forfend that we should assume that we are perfect, or that the British people are better than all others. But in this moment a certain clairvoyant makes us sure that we have been chosen by Providence for a role which we have not altogether deserved, and from which we would shrink if there were any other way to save our souls. Over and over again each one of us has unconsciously said, "If it be possible let this cup pass from me."

A traveller late at night heard a cry in a garden. He found a great Cross and a man nailed upon it. He tried to unfasten the ropes and drag out the nails driven through his hands and feet. But the victim said to him, "You can't move me till the whole world comes to take me down."

Then he knew who it was.

40

The Soldier's Religion

IN THE EARLY DAYS OF CHRISTIANITY the Church took no interest in the things of the world, but from the very earliest times there were Christians in the Roman army. One cannot easily forget our Lord's beautiful tribute to the centurion, and in all the ages of Christianity there have been devoted followers of Christ who did not think that their profession was incompatible with their religion.

The spirit of the Crusades colored mediaeval history, and in our own English story there are many names of Christian soldiers which occur to us—Philip Sidney, Henry Havelock and Gordon of Khartoum. A great mistake which civilian Church people often make is to imagine that a soldier is different from the ordinary man. No doubt in the stern school of war men see both good and evil, and in the great world war no one who came through those years in the trenches could ever be just the man he used to be. When chaplains wrote lyrical stories about the private soldier, one reason for their enthusiasm was because in civilian life they had never seen much of the average man—that is one of the tragedies of a clergy-man's life. The Canadian soldier does not reflect the views of a military caste, but the character of ordinary Canadian male humanity. What he thinks about religion and the Church is what young men generally think. His interests are those of his own generation.

124

First of all, let us be very candid. On the whole, the average man has not much respect for the Church. He does not belong to it and does not want to. It is true that most men have a formal connection with Christianity. They attend services for various reasons, but very often they are not much interested. They do not think of working for the Church; to go to a revival meeting would seem to them a grotesque thing to do. A somewhat aggressive soldier was once giving his opinion of the Church to his padre. Perhaps he was trying to be funny. He said: "The first time I went to Church they threw water on me; the second time I went they threw rice after me." "Yes," said the exasperated chaplain, "and the last time they will throw sand on you."

And yet the Church has given to most of us some vague knowledge of the Christian faith and imparted some elements of reverence and belief which will often bear fruit in later life. We have known many an excellent Church warden who has been recruited in middle age from this class.

One of the first lessons that a chaplain learns is that he has to live daily in the army in the light of the fact of the comparative failure of the glorious Church, of which he is the representative. He lives with a battalion of splendid male vitality and sees what a small place he holds in the lives of the majority. It must be confessed that the army itself is not very helpful in this regard. The chaplain is about the last person appointed on the strength. He feels lonely to begin with when he finds that, whatever men think of Christ, they require that he shall prove himself before he wins his right to their regard. Dimly, but really men realize what the Church might be, and that is why they are so contemptuous sometimes about what they see.

125

There is no hatred of Christ behind their indifference, for there is hardly a man to be found in whom, beneath his reserve, there is not a religion of some kind. Sooner or later all chaplains come to understand that the majority of men prefer to appear indifferent. They do not like religious service if they have any suspicion that it is only an army formality. Particularly the average man objects to the simplicity of coffee and buns being used as a prelude to what they call "a pep talk" about their souls.

It is certainly an education to live among soldiers. During the last war most chaplains heard enough swearing in a week to keep their hair on end for the rest of their lives, and sometimes they learned priceless home truths through mixing with soldiers when their tunics were unbuttoned, and if they were shocked their congregation probably took good care that they should witness plenty more. One of the favorite indoor sports in the canteens was the quiet baiting of parsons.

And yet they were, and are, such splendid fellows. Donald Hankey, who wrote "The Student in Arms," told the truth when he described how the average reticent, conventional citizen was amazed when some of the most unpromising men seemed to blossom into glory in the face of hardship and danger. At the time when he felt a cold chill in his stomach, these men were full of gayety and enthusiasm. Nothing daunted them. Barrage, bombs, cold and wet were all alike to them. They laughed, they sang, and underneath their unconventional speech there shone a spirit of invincible immortality.

And so, if we are wise, humble and just, we will ask ourselves, Why is it that conventional Christianity is not as popular in the army as it should be? Perhaps these men do not like the thing which they know as religion.

126

They look at the religious life as they think they see it and say: "We could not stick that." They look at the only religious people they meet and feel in their hearts: "We do not want to be like that." They find the Churches stiff and uncongenial, and they often find Christian people critical and uncharitable, and they do not find good comradeship in Church circles, and that is one of the things which they love most in life. Many a man thinks that if he ever became religious he'd have to say good-bye to all his chums and he would rather die than do that, for loyalty is to him the greatest thing in life; and, alas he only knows the stained glass window Christ, beautiful, gentle, mediaeval, apart from our modern world. But if men could only know the great Companion, if he could but see Him. In the words of Herbert Gray: "They have not seen the Jesus Whose life was never sombre but Who was possessed of a marvellous attractiveness for all such men as these; Who never withdrew from ordinary society however mixed; Who was not gushing but had the dignity of a strong man; Who was not effeminate but had in Him the constraining force of a great personality."

And if they have never seen Him, it is our fault; our preaching and our example have not set Him forth. Very few men like ministers; the clerical profession is not admired, and the professionally religious man is not a beautiful sight. It may be that there is a religion at the Front based on fear, but it is not common and certainly not admired. But if a man has character and a message, he may be a force incalculable in the life of a battalion or an army. In the British Army in 1915 there was a little padre named Studdert Kennedy, as Irish as Paddy's pig, with a face like a gargoyle and dark magnetic eyes. They called him Woodbine Willie. Suddenly it was discovered that he was a poet and a prophet, and whenever he spoke thousands laughed and wept at his words, and the hearts of men turned to him as a rose opens to the sun, for true religion is part of life. St. Augustine discovered that fifteen hundred years ago. "O God, Thou hast made us for Thyself, and our hearts can find no rest until they rest in Thee."

41

Greater Love Hath No Man

LOVE IS THE GREATEST THING in the world. Its supreme example was One who gave His life for mankind. We are living in an age when we cannot forget man's capacity for evil. Out of the depths of his primordial past the volcano has burst, and there seems to be a danger that all the spiritual values of life may be consumed. The soul cries out, "Oh, wretched man that I am! Who shall deliver me from this death?"

But love is stronger than death; sacrifice is greater than selfishness, for it is divine. Virtue is more mysterious than vice.

Why are men good? Why do we thrill to the heroic and fall in love with the beautiful? There is something in us which refuses to be satisfied with the materialistic scene.

> *Just when we are safest, there's a sunset touch,*
> *A fancy from a flower bell, some one's death,*
> *A chorus ending from Euripides—*
> *And that's enough.*

John Ruskin in a beautiful passage from his "Roots of Honor" discusses the sacrificial side of life. He says that the intellectual professions are related to the life of every civilized nation.

The soldier's profession is to defend it. The pastor's is to preach it. The physician's is to keep it in health. The lawyer's is to enforce justice, and the merchant's role is to provide for it. He goes on to say that it may become the duty of any man to die for his profession. The physician, rather than desert his patient. The lawyer, rather than countenance injustice.

During the present war we have learned that in darkest Europe men and women of all professions and of none have shown a spirit which is in accord with the highest ideals of humanity. In fact it is the glory of the so-called common people of England that, having few material possessions, they endured the bombing of London to save the world.

The soldier in wartime stands apart. He is the sacrificial man. If there ever was a time when the man in uniform was a careless adventurer, freed from the responsibilities of civilian life, it died during the last great war.

The young men of today did not make this war. That was the privilege and responsibility of the older generation. The tragedy of all war has been that it is the flower of each successive generation which is ruthlessly cut down. They go with songs into the battle. Their gaiety disguises the pain, the waiting and loss of those who would have been the leaders of tomorrow.

We are now approaching the decisive moment. Canada's long preparation is over. Four years ago thousands of boys went away. Now they are men. A full college training for a life's career. Many gallant deeds have been done, many decorations won. But the inner life of the soldier is not know to his countrymen.

A young officer left Canada after completing his

university course. He was a born soldier; an idealist, a leader and a scholar. He won rapid promotion. He served in Africa with the British Army as an observer, where he was slightly wounded. Returning to his unit, he went through the long trial of Commando training. One might have thought that such experience would make any one indifferent to the value of life.

One day, during intensive operations in prepared trenches, a young soldier pulled the pin of a live grenade and froze to the missile instead of throwing it. It was a four-second fuse. The trench was full of men. Death was at hand. Life was sweet. The officer did not hesitate. He knocked the petrified recruit down in the trench, ordered the others away and hurled the grenade, but it exploded just as it left his hand. He received the blast himself. Though terribly wounded, he stood erect and ordered stretcher-bearers for the man whose life he had saved. Then, telling his second in command to carry on, he thought of himself last of all.

Such a story in such a place is a call to see the image of God in man.

> *He was a gambler, too,*
> *My Christ:*
> *He took His life and threw*
> *It for a world redeemed.*
> *And e'er His agony was done,*
> *Before the westering sun went down,*
> *Crowning that day with its crimson crown,*
> *He knew*
> *That He had won.*

"Greater love hath no man than this, that a man lay down his life for his friend."

42

The Well of Bethlehem

THERE ARE SOME CHARACTERS in song and story who have the power of impressing posterity with something of the charm felt in their presence by their contemporaries. King David is the best-known figure in ancient history, save only Jesus Christ. He was not perfect, but he paid for his sins. Shepherd, warrior and poet, his magnetism makes him a human figure for ever. This is the man who loved Jonathan and spared the life of his mortal enemy, whose cry for a dead son clutches every father's heart after three thousand years.

The episode of the Well of Bethlehem is a picture of middle age. The Lion was trapped in a cave near his boyhood home. One afternoon, parched by the Syrian sun, he exclaimed: "O, that one would give me to drink of the Well of Bethlehem, which is by the gate." Three of his young staff officers cut their way through the ranks of the enemy and brought the cold, clear water to their chief. But he said: "Shall I drink of the blood of the men which went in jeopardy of their lives?" So he poured it out as a thankoffering to God.

Here is a story of today. Three years ago tomorrow the shadow of war descended on our world. We all remember the chill of the thought that freedom was about to pass away, and that we might never again breathe the air of men who could look the whole world in the face unsubdued and unafraid. A great sigh arose from the Empire: "O, that some one would bring us a draught from the old Well." It was dug by our ancestors centuries ago and deepened by succeeding generations. It had never seemed possible that our heritage could be denied to us until the bombs on London began to fall.

And so it came to pass that the sons of Canada stood up. For three long years they have joined with their brothers from other lands to keep the Ark of the Covenant. If we are breathing unpolluted air now, it is due to those who counted not their lives dear unto themselves. Our airmen have written the legend of Canada in the skies of every continent. Our seamen, many of whom never before saw the ocean, have kept the life line of the North Atlantic. The water of the Well of Bethlehem has been transmuted. "These laid the world away, poured out the red sweet wine of youth."

But until now Canada's Army overseas has been waiting and watching. Dieppe came the other day with the sudden shock of the Second Battle of Ypres on St. George's Day, 1915. We always knew, but now we feel that the gates of freedom are Gates of Pearl.

It was on such a summer day that David thirsted that the mighty men of Canada stormed the beaches of France. It was a deed of chivalry and sacrifice. It was an act which is full of mystical significance. In Toronto, Hamilton and other cities there are houses of mourning. The Cup of Ease which glistened cool and clear was turned red in our hands. Those who have died would not desire us to mourn unduly, for they are safe from the storms of our fitful life. The best way we can honor them is to use the precious gift they have bequeathed to us. Their sacrifice will not be in vain if we are stabbed awake to consecrate ourselves individually and as a nation to those Christian principles which we have praised but not followed.

The Well that the world needs is the Well of Bethlehem. It was dug in the night by the light of a star. The first cover of the well was a barn. The Shepherds, unable to sleep because the heavens were filled with music, came to see the opening of the Well. The Angels, at the first gush of its living waters, dipped their chalices of joy and sang, "Glory to God in the Highest, and on earth, Peace, Good-will to men."

43

The Women of England

THE OTHER DAY twelve representative Canadians who were returning from a month's tour in the Old Country sat down to ask each other what was the greatest thing they saw in the British Isles. It was an extraordinary surprise that the unanimous answer was, "The women of England."

On the other hand, a traveller from France who has lived in that country for twenty years described it as a land which is physically, mentally and spiritually sick, and still further said that one of the reasons for the fall of France was the fact that the women, who in the last war were the greatest inspiration of their men, had come to worship the Maginot Line. It was their influence which persuaded the country that anything, in the long run, was better than war.

The women of England in its long history have known what it is to grieve and weep for their husbands and their sons. One million British dead left three million broken-hearted womenfolk to mourn for them in 1918. But at the present time the women of England are an example to the womanhood of the world. The distinction between classes is rapidly fading. The uniform is a great leveller, and girls are learning to appreciate the qualities of their sisters who do not speak with their own accent. In some ways this is still a man's world. The big luxury hotels of England are able to circumvent the ration laws by serving game and other exotic food at lunches where women seldom go. Our hearts go out to the mothers of families in little towns and villages where no money can buy an extra pound of meat or a dozen eggs. A lady in Torquay received a tin of butter from Canada, and she got all her neighbors to come and look at the marvel. It was so beautiful that they couldn't bear to open the tin, and it was reverently put away.

We seldom think how the problem of the evacuation of women and children is very largely a feminine matter. It is hard on the poor mothers from the East End to give up the delights of the crowded streets, even though it is sometimes bombed. The conversation in the mornings with the lady in the next window as the blankets are shaken out for air is missed in the garden of Sussex, where flowers are not intended to be picked by the children and there is no one to talk to at night. The result is that if there has been no bombing for two weeks the refugees, without asking leave, find their way home. On the other hand, two maiden ladies living in a comfortable house are invaded by children whose knowledge of modern scientific sanitary arrangements is nil. It is not hard to imagine that to them there are some things which are harder to bear than danger or even death.

It was our privilege to see one of the most remarkable war plants to be found anywhere in the world. Two years ago wheat was ripening on the ground in the September sun. Today on this spot there is a town where six thousand workers are giving everything that they have to supply ammunition for the defense of civilization. It is a terrible tragedy that it should be necessary to do these things to conserve the treasures of the human spirit for ourselves and our children.

After passing through acres of wonderful workshops where the shining blocks of steel alloy were being fashioned into engine parts of indescribable beauty, and where hundreds of women, mostly young, stood confidently at the benches, working with the skill and enthusiasm of trained artisans, we thought that this must surely affect the characteristically feminine qualities of English girls, but at the noon hour we had the opportunity of seeing the greatest dining-room imaginable. Two thousand five hundred men and women sat down to a dinner that would have graced any restaurant. At the end of the great hall an orchestra made up of the personnel of the factory was playing, and a soloist who in happier days was well known in the Carl Rosa Opera Company thrilled every one with his voice. We saw a girl typically English, with curly yellow hair and blue eyes, sitting at a table reading a book, and wondered whether it would be a treatise on aero-engines. But when we asked to see the book we found it was a thriller entitled, "Passion in the Snows." There was a picture of an incredibly masculine Northerner in a fur parka embracing somebody who must have come from Devonshire, who seemed to like it. It would appear that girls are still girls, even in wartime.

A a matter of fact, this present war is a woman's as much as a man's war. All the precious qualities of womanhood—gentleness, sacrifice, romance and kindness—are the very things which are at stake. It is not too much to say that some of the divinest things in human life are the possession of a woman. She is the custodian from her very biological history of the things which Nazidom would destroy.

44

Coventry

DURING A VISIT TO ENGLAND a short time ago several Canadians had an opportunity to see the ruins of St. Michael's Cathedral, which was destroyed in the great raid of German bombers just a year ago.

During the present war the City of Coventry has become the sacrificial city of the Empire, and its glorious cathedral the sacrificial shrine. The Church and the bishopric date from the year 1100. The great tower was begun in 1373, and the slender spire was finished in 1433.

The stone of the building is of a pinkish-red color, and the oak beams came from the famous Forest of Arden, which covered much of Warwickshire a thousand years ago. Probably there was no city in England whose people have so passionately loved a building as this place which lived by commerce and yet regarded this spiritual sentinel as the symbol of its warrior archangel. The story of the tragic event is worth telling because it gave a new word to the German language and gave a complete demonstration of the wanton and senseless methods of the modern blitz.

For hours a continuous stream of enemy planes came in flocks and dropped their loads of incendiary bombs, returning for a new cargo, till all Coventry seemed on fire. The narrative comes from the lips of the Mayor of

138

the city, a sturdy, fair-haired Saxon, whose blue eyes gleamed like opals as he spoke. He is a well-known labor leader, with much of the cold steel of Ernest Bevin which has been such a strength to the Government of England during the last year. When the war is over, it is men like this who will have the last word when the terms of peace are decided.

It was the night of November 14. The Mayor said that in all his experience he had never known such bright moonlight. An attack was expected. The warning siren sounded at eight o'clock, and in a few minutes the whole horizon was ringed with light. In the cathedral four watchers were waiting, including the provost. They had been on voluntary service every night for a month. They had stirrup pumps on the roof and ladders ready. In the aisles below there were piles of sand. Unfortunately several bombs went through the soft lead and landed on the oak ceiling two feet beneath. It was impossible to lift the heavy plates, and soon the Church of St. Michael was doomed. When the fire brigade came, there seemed some hope, but before the hydrants and the hose were joined the great water mains were blasted. This was the real cause of the catastrophe. Nothing could be done. Dozens of men stood under the planes on the open roof and with their bare hands hurled the incendiary bombs over the battlement till they could do no more.

During the whole night the clock in the tower struck the hours. There were many at a distance who took this as a sign that their cathedral was intact. Even those who knew the worst were comforted by the calm notes sounding through the lurid night.

Today the tower stands as strong as ever. When the city burned, her Cathedral burned with her, just as when men suffer God suffers too. Yet the sight of that lovely spire all alone, soaring in the sky, is a promise of the eternal hopefulness of God.

We shall never forget our solemn procession through the ruins. The tall figure of one of Canada's pilgrims carried a wreath. On one side of him walked the Bishop of Coventry and on the other the doughty Mayor, wearing his gold chain and his face set like flint.

All the rubbish is cleared away. There is no vestige of roof, but the walls are intact to the clerestory. The stones seem molten into each other, and gleam a rosy red in the morning sun.

Some of us looked back, and the tall shaft of the tower seemed to smile. Where the altar once stood at the east end of the chancel, some inspired mystic had piled slabs of loose marble, and on top of it there was reared a jet-black cross made from two charred oaken beams lashed together.

> *O veiled and secret Power,*
> *Whose path we search in vain,*
> *Be with us in our hour*
> *Of overthrow and pain;*
> *That we—by which sure token*
> *We know Thy ways are true—*
> *In spite of being broken—*
> *May rise and build anew,*
> *Stand up and build anew!*

45

The Magnetism of Sacrifice

THERE IS NO DOUBT that success has an attraction for all kinds and conditions of men. Not only does it intoxicate those who have achieved it, so that the story of most conquerors has been a process of degeneration, but the spectators of the world drama are in danger of the fascination which makes the rabbit unable to move as the rattlesnake prepares to strike. During the last few months there has been a tendency for men and nations to throw moral considerations overboard. The history of the neutral nations in the present war does not make very pleasant reading. Most of them at heart were sympathetic to the ideals for which the British Empire reluctantly drew the sword. But we have all been taught to admire the victor. In athletics, business or politics "Vae Victis" is the motto.

At the present moment when the first act of the world tragedy is over and the curtain has fallen, we might well remember the terrible words of the philosopher William James: "The danger of moral flabbiness born of an exclusive worship of the bitch Goddess Success."

We venture to say that, in spite of popular opinion and what may seem to be the law of life on this planet, the spiritual power of mankind has a magnetism greater than all the ruthless might of sheer brutality. Still further, the experience of ages has shown that the great Christian virtues are really loved and admired only where those who try to practice them are in the throes of adversity.

We will take two examples. The first is from the long and varied career of the Church of Christ in the world. Every one knows that in the early centuries Christians were despised and rejected of men as their Master had been in the days when He lived among the great ones of the earth. But when Christianity was prosperous the seeds of its decay were sown. The institution of the lowly Nazarene who had no where to lay His head become the most stable and prosperous organization in a changing civilization. The arrogance of the leaders of all Churches became a legend, and so it came to pass that the Church was feared or hated by many who failed to see that the spots on the white robe of her divine purity were incidental to her pilgrimage in very muddy places.

Probably the nineteenth century marked the apotheosis of modern Christianity. But beneath the surface in every Christian land there were forces of rebellion. Our Christianity in the English-speaking world needs a new reformation.

Every one knows what has happened in the land of Martin Luther. It is said that Christianity is dead in Germany. But strange things are happening. The Bible Society tells us that the circulation of the Scriptures increased last year in Hitler's country by 100 per cent, and in the last five years more Bibles have been bought there than copies of "Mein Kampf."

Einstein has said that when the Nazi power began he looked to the universities to defend freedom. They failed. The literary men and newspapers were silent. Only the Church has stood squarely across his path. Here is a

142

tribute of affection and respect from one who was once an enemy.

The second illustration is one that touches every heart. The British Empire has had a long innings. She has influenced mankind for seven hundred years. She has been loved and hated by many, and now as the curtain rises upon the second act of this great spectacle she stands as a symbol of the dreams and hopes of millions in many lands.

The other day we saw an extract from a private letter written by Lady Russell, the famous author of "Elizabeth and Her German Garden." It speaks for itself:

Now about England. It is obvious, I think, that she has been cast by fate for the most glorious role of her existence. Whatever mistakes she has made in the past, and whatever mistakes she will make in the future, at this moment she is at the very peak of glory—a sort of twentieth century Christ taking the sins of the whole world on her shoulders alone and going to redeem us all; and even if she, her island, now goes under, it won't last, for she has her Empire, which will go on fighting till Nazi devils are finally scotched. We never let go, we shall never be slaves, and I'm so proud at this moment of being a bit of England that I find it quite difficult "not to burst."

46

The Miracles of Christ

THE DARK CATASTROPHE of the present hour has turned the minds of men in a surprising way to the possibility of Divine intervention in the affairs of this planet. After all, in spite of our superficial cleverness and our determination loudly expressed in the last century to rule our own lives without the meddling of God, we are only children. We remember the last sentence of a book which was published in England during 1918. A little girl was saying her prayers and she concluded as follows: O God, come quick, for Your king and country need You."

Christianity is a supernatural religion. If it had been only a philosophy or a system of ethics, it would long ago have been outmoded and forgotten. It takes for granted that there is a Divine Creator in whom we live and move and have our being, and that He has spoken to men in history, and in conscience, and that He is interested in the inhabitants of this minor star.

A miracle, from the Christian point of view, is not merely a freak exhibition of power. It must have some moral or spiritual significance. It is not enough to say that in a miracle God acts directly for once instead of leaving it to the laws by which He runs the universe. The old Christian writers did not think that all miracles were necessarily good; in fact Gregory the Great said that when the great tribulation should come upon the world Antichrist would show greater miracles, and for a time signs and wonders might be denied to the society of Christians. We wonder whether the great tribulation has come and whether these spectacular and unholy deeds of Hitler are manifestations of the Prince of Evil.

We will not argue with any one who does not believe in the miracles of the New Testament, for this would not be helpful, but for ourselves it seems that right is as incomprehensible now as it was when Job cried out to the Almighty from his bombed caravan in the desert. We have not time or strength to wander uncertainly amid its mazes, but, trusting God, we are ready to accept what neither we nor any one else can prove like a theorem of Euclid.

Of our Lord's many miracles we have records of only thirty-three, one for every year of His life, one for every month of His ministry. These can be divided into three classes: first, Jesus worked miracles in the realm of nature, and these are the ones that the modern man finds it hardest to believe—feeding the multitude with a handful of bread, quelling the storm by the magic of His words, raising the dead. In the calm and settled processes of the planets we can understand that there need be no intervention from the day that the morning stars sang together until the end of time they are inanimate and obedient, but when man comes into the picture, that wayward unpredictable child of the Divine, one can understand that here a Father's love might sometimes find it necessary to speak. After all, it would seem queer that the Almighty should shut Himself up in a universe that He could not control. A sign on a gas station to advertise brakes had these words: "If you cannot stop, don't start," and with all reverence we believe that God would never have created what He cannot ultimately control.

The second class of miracles associated with Jesus is the healing of the diseased and broken bodies of men. It is quite amazing to notice how much of His time the Saviour spent in caring for the work that the Red Cross is now trying to do. It is not hard to imagine where Christ is at the present hour—not far away from the bombed cities of war-torn Europe. And yet, in dealing with the solemn mysteries of pain and death, He did not put an end to disease or give immortality to our bodies as we know them. All who were raised from their beds died in due course; what He granted to them was what He grants to us—a brief postponement to show us that our time is in God's hands.

Finally, Jesus wrought miracles within the souls of men; His own disciples were different people when He had finished with them. He found a lunatic among the tombs and made him into a missionary. It was to miracles of spiritual healing that Jesus gave supreme importance, and it is this aspect of the Divine power in human life which will ultimately redeem the world.

47

Christ's Gentleman

ACCORDING TO WEBSTER'S DICTIONARY, the "Meek" are those who are mild of temper, not easily provoked, patient under injuries: and Christ says, Blessed are all men of that kind, for they shall inherit the earth.

The subject of the first two Beatitudes is as wide as the broad earth itself. For the world is full of the "poor in spirit." Abraham Lincoln said that God must like them because He made so many. And the world is full of men and women who are mourning. No family is without its sorrow; no house without its vacant chair. But this case stands far otherwise with its benediction. Probably among the thousands who, at various times, heard Jesus utter these words, you could count on the fingers of one hand all who could lay any claim to that blessing.

For meekness is not a natural virtue. No man is born meek. It is one of the fruits of the spirit, and of all the fruits of the spirit I think this is the hardest to cultivate.

The original Greek word is "Praos," which means "gentle," but it was the word that the Greek warrior used in describing a bridled horse—one who, after pain or flogging, was still full of spirit and under control of a master mind.

We are told that Moses was very meek. But he was the

147

young patriot who one day saw an Egyptian flogging a Hebrew slave and it was a word and a blow with him that laid the tyrant bleeding on the sand. And this was the man who was coming down from the holy mount with the Ten Commandments and, in a fit of resurgent passion, he dashed them to pieces on the rocky mountain side. It took forty years to teach Moses to control his temper and curb his tongue.

The second reason for the fewness of the meek is that the great majority of people don't look upon meekness as a virtue at all. How ridiculous would this text look if it were framed and hung as a motto in a business office! How would it do as a slogan for gasoline on a city corner? Not quite the spirit of modern life, we fear.

Among the Romans patience under injuries was not regarded as a virtue, but as an infirmity. "Nemo me impune lacessit." "Touch me if you dare"—the motto of Rome and quite familiar in international affairs today.

In the French version of the New Testament there is an inspired translation which shows us the real meaning of this Beatitude: "Blessed are the debonnaire." It is Christ's description of what the world calls a gentleman. We are not talking about him who is a gentleman by accident of gentle birth, but the man who has come to possess, in some measure, the gentleness of Jesus. It is the highest type of gentleman.

Kind hearts are more than coronets,
And simple faith than Norman blood.

The gentleman is considerate of others. He does not insist on having the best for himself. He does not turn two seats together on the train while a woman with a crying baby in her arms is compelled to stand. He does
148

not seek to push others to the rear of the procession. He never inflicts needless wounds. He lightens his brother's burden when he has an opportunity.

The gentleman has a sweet temper. He does not give himself the luxury of flying in a rage and speaking his mind. There are so many of us who rather pride ourselves on being quick to blaze and let ourselves go.

The gentleman is humble-minded. He "seeketh not his own." He does not swagger. He does not tell the world how good he is or how much he has suffered or how many crosses he bears for others. He is "debonnaire." He has the child heart. He can forget himself.

The gentleman is courageous. He has the highest type of courage. He dares a terror before which the most lion-hearted quail. There is nothing of which the average man is more horribly afraid than of being thought a coward. But the meek man can look that terrible enemy in the face with quiet eyes because he longs to be like Him who "when He was reviled, reviled not again."

Let us look back for a few moments on the story of the planet, thousands of years before man appeared, in the days of the Pleiocene and Jurassic periods when the great monsters roamed in the swamps of the primeval world. It was the heyday of the ichthyosaurus and the pterodactyl. Some of them were as big as a house. Their armor was as strong as that of a war tank. Could any one with a mind, looking at the world then, say that they would not be the survivors of life on this planet? Their brain was about two ounces to the ton, and you will find their remains in the fossil heaps of Alberta and Mongolia.

The same thing is true among the nations. It certainly seems that the warlike nations should be counted on to inherit the earth. There have been all too many nations

149

in the past that were little more than beasts of prey. They ground the weak beneath their feet and grew rich and mighty through the shedding of blood. Where are they now? They have passed into the graveyard of buried nations. They committed suicide in a mad and futile effort to possess the earth.

48

The Conquest of Fear

IT IS VERY INTERESTING TO NOTICE how old religious words
have been supplemented by the new psychology. When
philosophy was reborn in the Middle Ages it used the
language of theologians; but nevertheless, there are some
good old Anglo-Saxon words which still remain when
people speak of the soul of man—and one of these words
is "fear."

Not long ago in a conversation in a Pullman car two
friends were discussing what seemed to be the two gods
of the modern world. They decided that they were money
and power, which are very much the same thing. Then
they asked what were the two devils of our age, but this
time they agreed that fear stood alone the great demon of
the modern world. Yes, it is the disease of the age.

Neurasthenia, in all its forms and disguises, is almost
wholly a disease of fear, "and fear hath torment." It takes
many shapes. If we close our eyes we can see a long
procession of people, weary and heavy laden, crouched
beneath the burden of their fears. So the question of our
Lord rings through our minds, "Why are ye so fearful,
O ye of little faith?"

First of all there is the fear of life. We dread what may
be in store for us—unemployment, poverty, pain and sickness, losing the thrill of mind and body, the unknown

experiences, the shadows and the headlands of the future.

Again there is the fear of self. As civilization becomes more complex men and women lose the power to be happy with themselves. That is one reason why the pioneer, in the old sense of the word, is almost extinct. There are many people who are actually afraid to be alone. That was a characteristic answer of the fisherman sitting on a wharf with his line dangling in the oily water. When he was asked what he was doing, he replied, "I sit and think, and sometimes I just sit."

Have you ever seen the person who must have the radio turned on all day, and often two different machines giving two different programs at once? The greatest weakness of civilization is that the fine, gregarious instinct of mankind, which began with the family, in the end becomes almost a disease.

The fear of our neighbors is a very real thing at the present hour. Men are afraid of each other; especially perhaps is this true of nations. Europe is in the grip of the monster fear. The future of civilization itself is at stake and there are many who cannot sleep o' nights.

John MacMurray in his "Freedom of the Modern World" points out that the two emotional attitudes through which life can be radically determined are love and fear. The first is the positive principle of life, the latter the negative principle of death. Fear is the great emotional force that kills action. The animal who is paralyzed with terror cannot even move, and a cold chill ices the blood. There can be no initiative when a man is afraid except the spasmodic digging into the funk-hole or the building of a shelter.

John, the beloved disciple, speaks about the remedy of

fear. How true his words are! "Perfect love casteth out fear because fear hath torment."

The reason why men love the Psalms so much is because they picture universal experiences. "I sought the Lord," says David. "He heard me and delivered me from all my fears." It doesn't matter where a man lives or how he dresses, his heart, his hopes and fears are still the same. David may have dressed in Oriental robes, the Crusader in shining armor, Dr. Johnson have worn a powdered wig, the modern man a business suit, and yet every one of them has known what it is to be afraid.

The Christian religion has shown us how to conquer fear. The first two words of the angels' message are, "Fear not." Christ was born to banish fear. That old pagan world was engulfed in fear before He came—fear of God and fear of man. It was the Saviour who taught men that love is stronger than death. What a world it would be if we could rid ourselves of fear! The forts and armaments of nations would rust in ruin. Classes and individuals could clasp hands if suspicions were cast out.

In conclusion, there is the fear of death which exists in every creature which has imagination. Sometimes it becomes stark madness. Sometimes it is painted with poetry, as in Hamlet's soliloquy, which speaks of "that bourne from which no traveller returns." But here it is that Christ comes into His own. He was one Traveller who did come back, and His first words to us was "Rejoice!" Why should God look after our entry into this world and not look after our entry into the next? We should trust Him—"If it were not so I would have told you."

49

The Hills of Life

MR. LLOYD GEORGE AT THE BEGINNING of the Great War in 1914, in the Queen's Hall, London, in a speech which rang around the world, used a parable from the scenery of Wales, his native land, to illustrate spiritual truths. He showed how the languid and peaceful valleys were surrounded by mountain peaks where the air was keen and cold. "And so, he said, "this generation must climb from the secure valley of peace where our forefathers dwelt so long to the mountain peaks of endurance and sacrifice." And to those mountain peaks we climbed twenty-five years ago, but, when it was over, instead of returning to peace we descended to the slough of despond and disillusionment—but that is another story.

There is no doubt that Mr. Lloyd George kindled his imaginative picture of his own mountains from the genius of the ancient Psalmist who sang more than three thousand years ago, "I will lift up mine eyes unto the hills from whence cometh my help."

For Palestine is pre-eminently a land of hills. In the first place, its northern boundary is marked by the sun-capped peak of Hermon, which, in the clear Syrian air, may be seen from every corner of the Holy Land. It is not difficult to understand how, to the ancient people of God, the hills of their native land became a symbol of the aspirations of the human soul. For there are hills everywhere, large and small. When, at sunset, you stand at the site of ancient Jericho, deep down in the canyon of the Jordan, you look up on every side to the battlements of God. Eastward are the great purple ranges of Gad and Reuben from where Elijah, the Prophet, descended with the thunders of God. Westward, against the saffron sky, are the ridges of Judea, where Amos saw his visions, and, far away, the dim shadow of the Galilean hills from which Jesus of Nazareth came. Yes, we have a message from the ramparts of the Eternal to man in this present hour.

It is a strange thing that man is the only animal who naturally looks upward. Any one who has tried to train dogs or horses knows how incredibly stupid they are in discerning any outline above. The truth is that man naturally aspires.

It may be asked whether these hills of life are not a mere phantom. Sometimes when passing through the Canadian Rockies, as the eye looks up to the snow peaks and the sun shines upon the clouds that hang like a silk veil on the shoulders of Mount Robson, you wonder whether the whole thing may not be an illusion—and so it is with the spiritual world. Religion is certainly very beautiful, hanging as it does mysteriously above us, and touching the earth with all the light of our deepest longings. We would like to be sure that it is true.

There are three tests of mountains. The first is memory. When you have climbed a mountain it is part of your life forever. You could draw a picture with your eyes shut.

Again, the mountaineer is made by his mountain. It makes his climate; it moulds his character. No men who have lived among the mountains have ever been slaves, and so it is with the Mountain of the Spirit.

And, last of all, a man may climb a mountain for himself. Moving pictures or a guide-book are no substitute for exercise, and men do not generally reach the heights of life without discipline.

Religion does not attempt to justify its presence in the world. It comes forth in the silence like a mountain through the lifting mists. All the strong things of the world are its children, and whatever strength is summoned to its support is that which its own spirit has called into being.

50

In Praise of the Moon

THE SUN IS LIGHT, HEAT, AND LIFE. It is the most dominant material influence on this planet and on others also. The stars are a dazzling mysterious legend. They are either the greatest delusion of the human mind or the greatest exercise ever attempted.

The moon is the Cinderella of the heavens. We see its shadows and its seams. It is too near for complete idealization. It was the primer of the earliest ages, when childlike men first observed it wax and wane. Somehow we have always thought that the genealogies of Methuselah and his contemporaries indicate that primitive man measured his life by months instead of years. One of the most lovely prose poems in the world is enshrined in that ancient divine law book called Deuteronomy. Moses was a warrior, statesman. In his requiem of his age, the man who led a nation through the wilderness counts the blessings as his day draws into eventide. He has seen many suns, and the stars remain steadfast. But he also remembers "the precious things put forth by the moon."

The gifts of the moon are the consolation prizes of Life. They are not gold, but silver. They do not grow in a day, but are the unearned increment of the love of God, who understands our eager dreams and our tendency to disappointment and despair.

The lesson of the moon is true in the realm of the mind. Man in his most dynamic hours worships the light of the sun. Mind is everything. Logic is the solution of every problem. But the clear light of truth is like the sun on a snowfield. Too much exposure makes you blind. Sleep and rest bring balance and sanity.

Every one today is drawing a picture of the brave new world. It is taken for granted by most people that it is something new in human experience. We remember, however, an event 25 years ago which will some day be given its proper place in history.

At brigade headquarters in a little village called Jemappes, between Valenciennes and Mons, one morning a document was posted containing President Wilson's Fourteen Points. The paper was written by an idealist across the ocean, which was then five times wider than it is now. War-weary soldiers looked at it, and some wiped away a tear. The Belgians and Germans (who saw it later) wept unashamed. It seemed like a voice from Heaven. The author had a clear mind. There was nothing wrong with his principles. . . . Three months later he was stripped of his shirt and reputation at the poker table in the many-mirrored chamber of Versailles. The bright sunlight of knowledge was not enough to save the world.

In the sphere of emotion, the lesson of the moon is more striking still. The popular conception of love is that it belongs only to the morning of life. The sun is strong, the day is young, and passion has its hour. It is perhaps the great creative miracle of life. Years roll on. Toil, sorrow, pain touch the chords of existence. The time comes when the Moonlight Sonata has its turn. We grow nearer to those we love, because we have laughed and cried at the same time. What an odyssey life is.

> John Anderson, my jo John,
>   We clamb the hill together,
> And mony a canty day, John,
>   We've had i' ane anither.
> But we maun totter down, John,
>   But hand in hand we'll go,
> And sleep together at the foot,
>   John Anderson, my jo.

The moon shines with a reflected light. In the spiritual world there are many so constituted that they cannot look with unveiled eyes upon the majesty of God. Like the sun, He is too bright. They are awed by the brilliance of His purity and glory. So it has come to pass that the mystery of the Incarnation is the central fact of the Christian Religion. No wonder the most philosophical and mystical of the Evangelists, in attempting to describe the influence of Christ on his contemporaries, wrote: "The light shineth in darkness, and the darkness could not absorb it."

That has been the story of Christianity for nearly two thousand years. The influence of one who was God, and brought sunlight to a dark world tempered by the form of man, has never waned. It has the power of making those who have been lighted to shine for others. We all live on borrowed light. The true tragedy of our present world despair is that "The moon is down."

51

The Climate of Religion

EVERY LIVING THING IS INFLUENCED by climates. Religion is not to be found in a vacuum. Our spiritual life is very sensitive, and responds to the intellectual and moral climate in which it grows, a kind of atmosphere in which it breathes. We all have our private lives, but they are influenced by the world of ideas and habits and conventions which is very likely not of our own making and not under our own control. We are children of our age; we absorb the likes and standards of our time. In other words, we are the product of tendencies which may have been at work for centuries.

There was a time—at least for nearly a thousand years —when our ancestors lived in a world in which Christian ideas formed the foundation of all their life and thinking. Men took God seriously. They felt that their life here was only the first stage. They did not worry much about the world in which they lived. That was partly because they were too ignorant to take care of their bodies. They were very certain that there was something more important than the body. They called it the soul, and they believed that the true end of life was to prepare for an immortal life where they could fulfil their vision of God.

The time came when Man's whole balance of interest shifted; he gained a new view of the world and his own mind; he gained new powers; he discovered and invented and made himself master of everything except himself.

160

In the meantime he lost a good deal of his own view of God and of his own destiny. So it has come to pass that even the Christian Church has been influenced by the climate of our modern Babylon.

We are all thinking of a new world. Every newspaper and secular journal is filled with articles telling us of the contribution which science and medicine and economics are going to make to the new age. When the Christian ventures to say that we ought to count God as a factor in the future, and that Christianity might be expected to help, he is told: "You Christians will not have anything to do with this; this is our turn and our job." But the Church can never be Catholic until it is militant; as long as it is merely an ambulance picking up those who drop out in the march of our murderous civilization to nowhere in particular; as long as it limps behind the tanks and picks up the bodies, then we are going to go on quarrelling.

The time has come when organized Christianity must remember its mystic message to the souls of men. Jesus Christ is often called the Great Physician. We would do well to remember His words: "Seek ye first the Kingdom of God, and all these things shall be added unto you."

We agree with the words of Lewis Milligan in an article in the Tweed News last month, who says: "The preacher who substitutes socialism for the gospel is not only misrepresenting Christianity, but is holding out false hopes of a heaven in this life to mortal beings. Here we have no continuing city, but we seek one to come, said St. Paul, and it is as true for Christians today as when it was first uttered. Nothing short of immortality can satisfy the yearnings and aspirations of the human soul, and until preachers are obedient to the heavenly vision and authoritatively declare the gospel of Eternal Life, their preachings will be in vain and the Churches will be empty." Where there is no vision the people perish, and they are perishing from spiritual starvation.

The hungry sheep look up and are not fed,
But swol'n with wind, and the rank mist they draw,
Rot inwardly, and foul contagion spread;
Beside what the grim wolf with privy paw
Daily devours apace, and nothing said;
But that two-handed engine at the door
Stands ready to smite once, and smite no more.

Milton wrote that against the ecclesiastics and poets of his day who had no spiritual message for the people. "Milton, thou shouldst be living at this hour," for we have lost that "inward happiness" that comes with a consciousness of immortality. We have forfeited the vision of the Eternal for an economic plan and political mirage.

To tell the truth, it is clear that we cannot play with the Christian faith much longer. Human nature is at the end of the trail. There is a story in the 15th chapter of St. Luke's Gospel, which is called by St. Bernard "The Pearl of Parables." It has only 517 words. You can read it aloud in three minutes.

It tells of a boy who left home to have a good time. It is really the story of our Western Civilization for the last 300 years. We remember the point where the Prodigal comes to himself and faces the facts. He seems to say: "This is a beastly hole; I am tired of eating with swine. I am beginning to develop a snout myself. I hear they are going to ration husks next. It is about time I went home." Then he thought of his Father and the home on the hill. That is where our modern world stands today.

52

Portrait of St. Paul

AMONG THE GREAT MEN of 2,000 years ago there is scarcely one who lives so vividly as the first world missionary of the Christian Church. The main facts of his stormy career have been written by a contemporary who was his friend and Boswell. A collection of his letters to little communities which he visited are self-revealing to an extraordinary degree.

Alone among the first followers of Christ he seems alive. They are shadowed by their nearness to their divine Master. St. Paul comes into the story a little later, and we can study him without an aureole. His pecularities are so sharp and human that he has been spared the dangerous honor of complete idealization. That was true in his lifetime and also in history. His positive theology has repelled some people, who accuse him of distorting the historic Jesus. The sentinel Renan could never understand or appreciate the "ugly little Jew." We have many hints from his own writings and elsewhere that he was not a heroic figure. At Athens they called him a "cock sparrow," when he and his companion visited Lystra. The villagers picked the stately Barnabas as Jupiter, and Paul as Hermes because "he did the talking." Orientals thought that silence was the mark of a great god or a great man.

He was handicapped for years by some mysterious ailment which he calls "a thorn in the flesh." Some think it was ophthalmia, very common in the East. Lightfoot says that it is evident that the malady had three characteristics. It made the patient contemptible to others, it caused weakness, and was recurring. Malaria, which is endemic in Asia Minor, seems the most likely guess. Tradition pictures him as a sturdy little man, with a long beard, and bald. The early Roman portrayals of Peter and Paul are significant. The first is tall and commanding, with the simple dignity of a senator. He always holds the key as his symbol. The latter is less impressive, but invariably carries a long sword.

Paul was a vivacious personality, with a tendency to tumbling words when moved. He had native dignity which carried him on equal terms before governors and military commanders. In writing he was a slow starter, but no one ever exceeded him in the witchery of words. In his greatest moments he is intoxicated by his thoughts. His wit flashed like a rapier, but he had little sense of humor. He was essentially a man of the world. He knew the Arena and a soldier's uniform, and rather too much about the law. His illustrations of the sacrifice of Christ from legal analogy seem forced and unsatisfying. He does not seem to understand women, which is probably why he is not their favorite saint.

His conversion is one of the turning points in the history of the world. To him it was nothing less than a new birth. The memory of the Damascus road never left him. He was "a man in Christ" forevermore. The personal communion with his Saviour lifted him to a new plane. Every one knows that he had hated Christians and their Lord. Like many religious fanatics before and since, he had a cruel streak in him. In fairness it must be said that after he had seen the light he tortured himself more than others had ever suffered from his hands. He had a long time of discipline before God could use him. It is a mistake to imagine that Saul the persecutor became a perfect instrument of God overnight. On the contrary, he spent two whole years as a hermit in the Arabian Desert. He probably learned more of the ways of God there than he ever told.

The romance of Paul's response to Christ's love for him is the secret of his life. It was partly unconscious. The famous chapter of First Corinthians is not a poem on an abstract quality. It is a portrait of Jesus by a lover. Paul was only a voice pleading with the whole world to look at the beauty of the Saviour of men. It is a picture for the ages.

This man was a world figure—a master of thought and a king of action, the ideal missionary, a supreme theologian, but greatest as a lover of Christ, for "the greatest of these is love." "Who shall separate us from the love of Christ? Shall tribulation, or distress, or persecution, or famine, or nakedness, or peril, or sword? Nay, in all these things we are more than conquerors through Him that loved us. For I am persuaded, that neither death, nor life, nor angels, nor principalities, nor powers, nor things present, nor things to come, nor height, nor depth, nor any other creature, shall be able to separate us from the love of God, which is in Christ Jesus our Lord."

53

The World of Books

THE TIME HAS COME when something should be said in defense of books. The extraordinary acceleration of the tempo of modern life has streamlined everything to do with the mind of man. It has been pointed out that history may be learned from moving pictures, and the modern radio pours out a stream of knowledge which is free to all. Nevertheless, there is something to be said for the old-fashioned labor, whether of agony or pleasure, associated with one of the oldest arts of mankind.

We knew a man who lived for many years on the shores of Hudson's Bay, seven hundred miles from the nearest railway station, where letters came only twice a year. When the long missionary journeys in the summer were over he camped in a log house on the banks of the Albany River, in sight of the frozen sea. The pine trees stood frozen on the banks; the snow was four feet deep, the ice solid in the river, and at night the stars hung like golden beads from the rosary of heaven. And when the north wind howled and the doors were shut and the blinds drawn and the fire blazing in the stove he was never alone.

The heroes, the kings and queens of all the ages have been with him in that solitary room on the river's edge. He heard Tennyson and Kipling sing for him at his own fireside. He saw Hamlet and Julius Caesar moving majestically through the room. How wonderful the spirit of Shakespeare, the greatest Englishman that ever lived!

> *The poem hangs on the berry bush*
> *Till comes the poet's eye,*
> *And all the world is a masquerade*
> *When Shakespeare passes by.*

He travelled with Nansen on his immortal journey furthest North. He met Livingstone under the acacia at Ujiji. He was transported with Macauley to the great hall at the Westminster to see the trial of Warren Hastings. He knew those people better than many of the friends who lived for years afterwards in the same city block. They are real—far more real than many of the passers-by on Main Street on a summer evening.

No one can read all the books. It is not necessary that one should do so. When we go into a department store the first thing that strikes us is the number of things that we do not want, and among all the millions of books that are written very few will give us all that we need to know.

Read a great history like Green's "Story of the English People," which tells the romance not of kings and queens but of the common people and their struggle to liberty. Or, if you want a modern history, read "The World Crisis," by Winston Churchill, the greatest prose that has been written on the war. Those four volumes will give the author a place in English history to match his life of action.

Read great biographies like Morley's "Life of Gladstone," which is a picture of the Victorian age, the greatest in English history. The study of a character like William Gladstone itself is enough to stretch the mind and make us see what life is for.

Read a great adventure like Lawrence's "Revolt in the

167

Desert," surely the most amazing achievement of all the histories in the Great War.

These are things worth while, and, no matter what your life is or your work, they will touch with romance and glory the spirit of your leisure hours.

Among all the books that have been written, there is one which stands alone. The word Bible means "The Book." From every point of view it deserves that title. Millions of copies are circulated all over the world in five hundred languages every year. Every one thinks that he knows the Bible, and yet very few read it as they should. There has been so much written about the Bible that there are some whose knowledge of the Book is only second-hand.

Bruce Barton, in that interesting book of his called "The Book That Nobody Knows," refers to this fact in his introduction. He tells the story of some woman who approached a Bishop anxious to get him to talk on religious matters. She obviously knew nothing of her subject, and she said to him: "Bishop, is not the Bible wonderful? What is your favorite story?" He looked her straight in the eye and said: "I like that tale of Eliza crossing the river on the ice." "Yes," she answered, "isn't it wonderfully sad!"

The Bible needs no defense. Where in the world can you find stories like those of Joseph and David? Where are there lyrics like the 23rd and 121st Psalms? Where does the ocean roll of language touch the shore of the mind as in the matchless chapters of Isaiah? Carlyle once said in speaking of the Book of Job: "This is the greatest book that was ever written. It towers like a mountain peak above all the literature in the world."

For youth and age this magic Book has its appeal for joy and sorrow, too.

54

Why We Pray

IN THE DARKEST DAYS of the American Civil War some one asked Abraham Lincoln if he believed in prayer. The President answered: "There are many times when I have been driven to my knees because there was nowhere else that I could go." Human beings do many things which they cannot explain, the reason being that there is a certain intangible mystical quality in that part of man which distinguishes him from the lower animals. We are all aware that we belong for the time being to two worlds; one is the familiar world round about us. We sit in a motor car and drive up Yonge Street through a fairyland of Neon lights, but in the morning as we come down to the world of business it is very evident that it is a material world. Outside the window of our spirits we cannot see far, but memory supplies us with a knowledge of those things which are hidden from sight. Any attempt of man to escape from the material world where our feet are planted solidly on the pavement or on the grass leads to disaster. Man is not a disembodied spirit.

But there is another world. This spiritual world lies behind and penetrates our material existence, and sometimes it invades our earthly home. We belong to this spiritual realm, for we are spirits who know and feel and love; and just as we must take from the world of things food for our bodies, so in the world of spirits we search for what our souls require. We must come into touch with the Supreme Spirit and Creator of both worlds, and as the flowers reach up to the sun we must pray in order to live spiritually. Some one has said, "The more we pray, the better it goes," because prayer is the path by which we enter into communion with God.

This is a universal experience. The scientific method of reaching truth is not to reason in advance, but to go and see. Humans have always prayed. There have been cities without walls, there have been nations who have lived in the lonely desert without houses, but everywhere there has been prayer. Why, we cannot say. It is the dim, dumb instinct of the race; since the beginning of time man has felt that somehow, some time, somewhere some good will come of it. When we find a fin on a fish, or a wing on a bird, or instinct in an animal, it shows that it is not without method or purpose. The eye was developed in response to the existence of radiant light; the ear to tune with acoustic vibrations, and the soul to find its God. Coleridge has said that the act of praying is the very highest energy of which the human mind is capable.

It may seem strange to say that we pray in order to help God. Of course this does not mean that we think we can co-operate with God as with an equal, but it does mean that He whom scientists call the Great Cause, and Christians the Heavenly Father, has so limited His power that each man can choose whether or not he will work along with Him. We have to decide whether God can use us, and it is by prayer that this is done. "Our wills are Thine, we know not how, Our wills are ours, to make them Thine."

The miracle of prayer is the most priceless boon to our

humanity. There are, of course, theoretic difficulties, but they are torn to pieces by the instincts of humanity. Thistlewood, the Cato Street conspirator, cried, "O God, if there be a God, save my soul if I have a soul."

The science of prayer may be learned. The old mystics found the secret of the Most High because they waited in silence before Him. Too often we pray to God as if prayer were a monologue; we want to tell the Lord God instead of letting Him tell us. The modern phrase "A quiet time" is scientifically and spiritually true. There are many questions concerning prayer which are worth consideration.

Does prayer begin with myself? Is the effectiveness of prayer dependent upon the force and intensity of the one who prays? What is the heart of all prayer? These thoughts suggest to us what the saints of God have long known, that prayer is not an easy thing, but a very difficult thing, and yet the immortal story told by Christ concerning the Pharisee and the Publican shows us that the conventional and pompous self-satisfied ecclesiatic, in spite of his good opinion of himself, may be further away from God than the penitent sinner. The essence of prayer is that it should be simple and sincere. No un-inspired writer has ever illustrated this truth with more force than our own Shakespeare in his Hamlet. There the murderous, adulterous king kneels down to pray. It is not, we observe, that he is too bad to pray that he realizes that God will not hear him, but it is because he feels only remorse and misery and not repentance, and, although he remains on his knees, he soon finds that his prayer is but hollow mockery, and rising, he sighs aloud: "My words fly up, my thoughts remain below, words without thoughts never to Heaven go."

171

55

The Missionary

No study of the Canadian North is complete without consideration of the missionary. He takes his place with the explorer and the fur trader. It has been the fashion, in recent years, to speak contemptuously of the missionary. Amateur explorers and short-order tourists consider that it is a sign of sophistication to laugh at simple, guileless men and women who have tried to bring the message of Christ to foreign lands. From Charles Dickens to Somerset Maugham and Stefansson, this has been a popular touch for the home trade. It is true that the missionary work of the English-speaking world has seemed small in comparison with the pomp and circumstance of ambassadors, pro-consuls and trade commissioners—to say nothing of military glamour.

It would appear today that genuine Christian effort has been the most valuable investment the British Empire ever made. It might be also asserted that if one-half of the men and money spent for material prestige had been expended to further Christian principles on a free-trade basis our Christian civilization would not be fighting for its existence today. The French-Canadian voyageurs who penetrated the great Northwest by way of the Great Lakes carried the tradition of their Church with them. The missionary orders sent men and women who never returned. The bells and Church steeples far north of

St. Boniface are their monuments. During the Napoleonic wars the English Church Missionary Society was formed. For more than a hundred years it sent men, who gave their lives, to the Indians and Eskimos in Arctic Canada.

The great Mackenzie is the heart of the country. The old-time missionary was an agile for life. He had nothing except his faith. He learned the language of his people and shared their lives. His wife went with him to share his hardships. We saw three memorial tablets to the children of a father and mother who gave their best years to the Loucheux Indians, in a little Church within the Arctic Circle. They must have left their hearts in that little churchyard on the Peel River. The Mission House became the centre of the community. The home was a pattern for Indian women. In most cases the wife's lot was more restricted than her husband's. One thinks of the famous tribute of Joseph Choate to the Pilgrim Mothers. Because they endured all that their men did, and, besides that, they had to endure the Pilgrim Fathers!

It is worth while asking ourselves why men go to far-away places and live laborious lives. Very few people have gone into the subarctics of Canada with the deliberate intention of living and dying there. Many have died before their work was done, or because they could not get back. Some men have gone to find fame for themselves and honor for their country. The fur traders as a rule had no intention of remaining in the land where they made their wealth. For the Northwester there was the dream of a home in Montreal, and for the Hudson's Bay Company chief factor a pension and a Scottish village.

"The nameless men who nameless rivers travel,
And in strange valleys greet strange deaths alone,

The grim, intrepid ones who would unravel
The mysteries that shroud the Polar Zone . . ."

The old-time missionary was more like a sourdough than a trader or an explorer. The gold miners in the great days of '98 were looking for treasure—not a respectable competence, but wealth beyond avarice. It was that yellow gleam that led them in thousands down wild rivers where the boat was smashed and they burned it to save the nails and build a boat again. They were all half-crazy, according to conventional standards. Robert Service tells a story of an old miner who followed a trail across the tundra sponge to a mountain which shot from a crater of pure radium all the colors of the rainbow, like the combined searchlights of the navies of the world. It was the Pool of the World's healing, and he promptly staked his claim. These servants of Christ whom we call missionaries believed that they were called for a high purpose. "They had staked the Northern Lights." The souls of the Indians and the Eskimos were to them God's precious jewels. They wanted to bring news of Jesus to the children of the North. If that is madness, then 'tis folly to be wise.

56

The Mystic Stairs

POPULAR RELIGION IN MODERN DAYS deals with men in the mass, but, after all, when we stop to think, we know perfectly well that the reason why the Churches have failed and theology has little effect on the lives of men is because the individual soul must make its peace with God. The craving of the human heart for the stillness and strength of eternity is universal.

In a medieval poem we remember a reference to mankind "lying on the world's great altar stairs that slope up to God." It is a haunting picture of man trying to find courage for that journey which every soul must make.

In the last part of Dante's great poem, when he begins the ascent to Paradise, there are three steps which mark the stages of his climb. First, there is a step of pure white marble; that kind of whiteness which is only to be found in the marble of Italy and Greece—heaven's contrast to the blue sky and the dark sheen of the green pines.

The second step is a startling and unpleasant surprise. Rough, broken and uneven, it looks like a piece of cement or lava.

And the third step is a flaming porphyry—that frozen fire to be found in the pillars of the Church of St. Sophia at Constantinople which were purloined by Justinian from Baalbek's Temple of the Sun.

These three steps to the Hill of God are not only dramatic but they are true to human life. If we want to climb the Mountain of the Spirit, this is the only way we can begin. Any other track, however alluring, will never lead us to the summit.

The meaning of the poet's imagery is this: When any man or woman would draw near to God it is necessary to begin with the white step because this is the symbol of purity and sincerity. It's the same idea which is found in the white robe of the Book of the Revelation. First of all we must be clean, but our own washings will never prepare us for the presence of God. For no one can take his conscience to pieces and put the screws on the shelf as if he were cleaning a motor car. The fact is that the essence of Christianity is to be found in the belief that we can't make the first step ourselves without the grace of God. "Lord, if Thou wilt, Thou canst make me clean."

From the white marble we pass to that strange unlovely and unpolished stone. It is a shock, but it is true to life. It is the broken and contrite heart. Some people may doubt that vital penitence comes after the cleansing, but, when we consider the matter, we'll see that it is impossible for one to understand the character and the guilt of sin until the cleansing Spirit of Christ has touched the heart. It is the new day which makes us see how shabby is the room into which we invite Him, who is the "Light of the World." The whole philosophy of conversion is challenged here. It is a great mistake to think that when man has once turned his face toward God he will never have to fight any more.

And, finally, there is the step of that incredibly red rock, which has to be seen to be believed. It is the red glow of sacrificial love. "We love him because He first loved us," and it is on this third step that the Christian finds that peace and joy which the world cannot give and the world cannot take away. This is the real meaning of that ecstasy which is part of the hidden life of the great Saint of all ages. They are of various types. John Bunyan, the Puritan, has written in words that warm the heart like fire. His dress, his education and his manner of speech were all opposite to the life of St. Bernard of Clairvaux, and yet they both knew the Heavenly City. They had seen it from afar and their hearts opened to its passionate flame.

57

Is Christianity Dying?

IT IS QUITE COMMON THESE DAYS to hear people say, with the air of subdued satisfaction with which we relate the misfortunes of our friends, that Christianity is finished. It is worth while to consider this somewhat alarming suggestion.

The Christian Church, to any sympathetic observer, is a heartbreaking institution, and Christians themselves are more aware of this than any outside critics can possibly be. Bishop Lightfoot of Durham once said that history is the best cordial for drooping spirits. He was probably thinking of the long and checkered history of Christianity.

To go back to the very beginning, we remember that in the days of our Lord Himself a wise old leader of the Jewish Church gave advice to certain hotheads who were anxious to start a persecution. What he said may have been cynical, but it was very shrewd. "Gentlemen, leave Christianity alone. If it is false, it will die of itself, but, if it should be from God, nothing that you can do can stop it."

About A.D. 178 a famous Greek philosopher of great culture named Celsus wrote what he called "a true word," which he intended to be the last word about the fantastic rise and fall of this new religion. And even earlier than that the historian, Tacitus, about A.D. 100, in his Annals, thought it worth while to explain to posterity what the religion and superstitution of Christ had been. As a matter of fact, the Church is always dying, to appear again with renewed vitality in the next generation. The ebb and flow of religion is almost as regular as a tide. During the Middle Ages the birth of the great religious orders came time after time to bring hope and healing to a world that was painfully struggling to change itself into the form of our modern civilization. There were many who thought in the eighteenth century that reformed religion was virtually doomed. Instead of that there came the surprising flowering of the nineteenth century.

Today, of course, every thinking man knows that Christianity is fighting for its life. But it is by no means dying. It may well be that the world is on the eve of such a religious reformation as it has never known. There is a book which has been written by Prof. C. B. Martin of McGill University. He is an anatomist and has lived with teachers of science all his life, but he knows something about the spirit of man and he writes vigorous and convincing English prose. We were very much interested in his analysis of the decline of religion in modern times. We are reminded somewhat of the five causes which Gibbon gives for the spread of Christianity at the first, in a famous chapter of his "Decline and Fall of the Roman Empire." Professor Martin says that the first enemy of the Church is the extraordinary rise and progress of modern science. We can all admit this. There is no doubt that from the days of Darwin a new spirit arose among thinkers which was critical of if not destructive to the mystical conception of life. It is true that in the exuberance of the first discoveries some scientists said very harsh and contemptuous things about all religion, but, unless we are mistaken, in recent years the leaders of English science are beginning to admit that there may be something more than matter in the cosmos after all.

The second enemy of religion, according to the writer, is that it involves a "lot of sham and make-believe," and is infected by a bad spirit which he and others would call ecclesiasticism. And, thirdly, there is the greatest enemy of all, a fear widely felt that the existence of pain and evil in the world must mean one of two things—either that God does not exist or that He does not count. These observations cannot be ignored.

Nevertheless, in spite of this fact we feel that, in an age that largely despairs of progress and is completely disillusioned about all political experiments, Christianity is the only hope of the world. It has saved mankind before, and if it cannot do so now nothing else can. It would be a tragic thing, indeed, if some historian a thousand years from now should say: "It was because the men of that day would not listen to Christ that civilization collapsed and a dark age set in."

Canon Barry of Westminster pleads with passion and fire for faith in the future. Here is what he says: "As we watch the triumph of the human spirit matching itself against such desperate odds, we know we are living in a new dimension. We are learning anew that the eternal order is man's native climate and his home."

58

'The Christian Headache'

THE EXISTENCE OF EVIL is the oldest and the most difficult moral problem of mankind. In this moment of world turmoil it shrieks to high heaven. From the days of Cain and Job voices have challenged the Almighty to justify His ways with men.

Christianity is the modern target for all the critics of the moral government of the world. It is no wonder, when we think of the deliberate extirpation of the Jewish race, who gave Christendom its knowledge of God. Last Christmas, while the radio was broadcasting "Holy Night," there were Jewish children going to their deaths in sealed cattle cars in Poland, their lungs poisoned with the unslaked lime with which the floor was strewn, and with the dead standing upright because there was no room for them to fall. In what scale will the president of the immortals weigh that ghastly deed?

The problem of evil is a triangle because all consideration of it starts not from one point, but from three: First, there is the axiom of the absolute sovereignty of God. He is the Creator of heaven and earth. His will sustains and orders all things. The second point of the triangle is that God is love, purity and wisdom. If He were anything else He would not be what we mean by God. The third is the apex of the triangle. The two others converge on it. There is evil in the world: the terrible fact of physical, moral horror. Here is the Christian's intellectual crucifixion. His feet are tied to the base and his hands to the arms of a cross.

There are three theories which Christian philosophy rejects. The first is the old classical idea of Fate, that everything that has happened or will happen is fixed from the foundation of the world. All that we do or are, all our hopes, fears, joys and sorrows have been rationed to the last ounce. Freedom, therefore, is an illusion. The cold logic of such a solution is a nightmare. There is a story told of a certain Dutchman—Robbertz—who was being harried by two theologians about the origin of sin. He said: "When the first sin was committed Adam put the blame on the woman, and the woman put the blame on the serpent. The serpent, who was young and callow, made no answer. Now that he has become old and confident, he comes to the Synod of Dort, and says that God had done it."

The second classical way of explaining evil is to say that it is an illusion. If God is perfection, of course anything He creates must be good; far be it from us to tell Him that there is anything wrong with His universe; so evil is only delusion of the mind. His doctrine leads to pantheism which identifies God with the world of reality. Unfortunately, we cannot get rid of all the grisly facts of the contemporary scene by regarding them as unreal. The martyrdom of China, the ten millions who have died under the pitiless Russian skies, the broken hearts of sorrowing wives and mothers . . . the starving, the wounded, the prisoners, like martyrs, who cry from beneath the altar, "How long, O Lord? How long?" It is a little too much to ask us to regard all this as an artistic, dark background to make the highlights of the picture shine in splendor.

Now for the final and most popular way of solving our problem. Can we blame the devil for all our trouble? Some say that there must be another creative will opposed to the will of God. This concentrates upon the brute fact of evil, and implies that God is not master in His own house. If we follow this thought to its logical conclusion, it simply means that there is dual control without any prospect of an armistice. No! If we believe in God at all, we believe in one God. Jesus prays that we may be delivered from the Evil One, but He also promised, "Every plant which My Heavenly Father planted shall not be rooted out."

Napoleon once asked an astronomer whether he did not think that the orderly procession of the heavens suggested the possible existence of God. Laplace replied: "Sire, I have no need of that hypothesis." Some of our modern philosophers have truly said that the problem of evil does not trouble one who does not believe in God. Evil will always be what it has been—a fact like the weather or death. Anything more pathetic than the accidental appearance of man, with all his dreams and his unique capacity for love and suffering, in a mindless and meaningless universe could not be imagined.

There is no answer to the problem of evil in purely intellectual terms. The very belief in God which creates and constitutes the intellectual riddle is turned to truth by the test of life. That is Newbolt's testimony in his lines on Clifton Chapel:

This is the chapel; here, my son,
Your father thought the thoughts of youth,
And heard the words that one by one
The touch of life has turned to truth.

59

Religion Makes the Front Page

IN THE EDITORIAL COLUMN of one of the most distinguished and beautifully written of our weekly papers there were two long paragraphs dealing with entirely different aspects of religion. The fact that the writer was icily impartial has nothing to do with the case. At least the Church got a headline, even though it was of a quasi-obituarial character, and to add to our surprise we read that a Canadian statesman about to leave our shores has announced that the Church has failed.

The Church, with its moralities, its standards and its dreams, has known strange changes of climate in its long history. Its triumphs, its sufferings, its failures and its recoveries are part of the romance of our human story.

In the editorial to which we have referred there was a reference to the subject of Sunday observance. While some of the theological sanctions may have lost their cogency, the fact remains that a day of rest is needed in our industrial civilization more than ever. By all means let the soul of man be free. Let the lover of nature find his soul in his own way, but let us not be deceived by a specious liberalism which continually, under various pretexts, try to rob man of his rest in order that somebody may have more chance to make money.

The second allusion refers to the decline of Theology

and it is based on an article in the Nineteenth Century. The distinguished Canadian commentator, in speaking on this subject, which is certainly not new, makes some very profound and true observations on the place of Theology in modern life. There was a time when Theology was the most popular of all subjects for the exercise of the human mind, to say nothing of the soul of man. Later, philosophy and science have taken pride of place.

It is specially noted that in our modern life, not only outside the Church, but in the Church, there is a decline in the emphasis of the fact of sin. The artificial phraseology of Christian doctrine, which is very largely based on Alexandrian Greek thinking, has become almost unintelligible to the average Christian of today, excepting in a few faithful fundamental churches which still speak the language of their forefathers.

But the writer points out with great shrewdness that this change of attitude toward sin, which was noted by Sir Oliver Lodge twenty years ago, has not brought happiness, although it is very often said that our fathers were terrified by the language of the pulpit, and innocent children clung to the pillars to keep them from sliding down to hell. Nevertheless, apart from the physical sufferings caused by war, tyranny and unemployment, the general level of happiness is certainly lower than it was before 1914, and this extraordinary fact also becomes apparent, that man, having escaped from the terrors of hell, has created for himself new devils under the modern inhibitions and neurosis. The old doctrine of Original Sin is very like the kind of thing that a psychoanalyst will be likely to tell a fashionable lady in his consulting room. In Theology sin is not an act; it is a disease.

185

As for the retired statesman's valedictory theme of the failure of religion, it seems to us that we have heard that observation before. The truth of the matter is that true religion never fails. Wherever it has been tried, it has transformed the life of men and nations. It has been found difficult, and for that reason men have too often refused to practice it. Christians may fail—they have often done so in the past—but Christ has never failed. One has only to look at this poor, hag-ridden world at the present moment, with its inspired genius for distorting the gifts of the Creator, to see that in the teaching of Christ still lies the hope of the human race.

60

Castles in Spain

St. Paul was one of the greatest adventurers in human history. If he had not been an Apostle, he would have been an explorer. His whole life was an odyssey. He proved that a saint can be a man of action. It was not for nothing that in the old Roman medallions he always carries a sword. He was one of those men who lived in storms, and yet at the very zenith of his life, in the closing words of his greatest Epistle, he says the most human thing which he ever penned: "Whenever I go to Spain, I shall be satisfied."

To any one who lived in his age in the Orient, Spain was a romantic dream. It was there that the ships of Tarshish went. Did he ever get there? We do not know. Church tradition says that he did, but it was very doubtful. But that does not matter; the value of a Spain is not that you get there, but that you keep its picture in your heart. Browning says somewhere: "A man's reach must exceed his grasp, else what is Heaven for?"

There never was a moment in our lifetime when the world needed a castle in Spain more than now. What that castle is depends upon the age, the character, and the temperament of the individual. Let us think for a moment of youth's castle in Spain. No boy wants to rest. If he dreams at all, it is of some great task that he wants

187

to accomplish, some position that he means to gain, some heroic dead which he is resolved to do; and it is a good thing that youth should dream. The age in which young men and women have no ideals is doomed. Our hearts go out to the young men of the Empire at the present moment who have thrown the world away and enlisted in the great adventure for the freedom of mankind. We hope they may find their castle in Spain, that they will achieve victory and return to read their history in a nation's eyes. But there may be some who, like St. Paul and his Master, will reach the consummation of their dream only through the gate of sacrifice and death. But it is not the length of life that matters; it is how that life is lived.

Then we think of those who are in the noonday of life's activity. They are a little bit shopworn, some of the early vitality has gone, but they know that they still can work; that there is still a job to do. They also have their castle in Spain, of a different kind. It is good to think of rest and retirement, to look forward to the day when we shall not be rushed by the demands of business, when our hours and days shall be our own, when we shall have time to read and think and pray. A little cottage in the country for our eventide, perhaps somewhere in the dear familiar locality of our childhood; very simple but with modern plumbing. There we shall answer all the letters that we have neglected. Here our friends will come to see us—maybe. Perhaps we shall never get there; it may be our lot to have our necks in the collar right to the end, but it is nice to think about it, and it helps us to carry our load.

There is nothing more beautiful than the castle in Spain of the aged Christians, those who are waiting for the

188

hope of a life complete in communion with God, where there is no more pain, no more age, no sickness nor death, and where they meet their loved ones who have gone before. Not a place of endless monotony and eternal song, but where "His servants shall serve Him and they shall see His face; and there shall be no night there, and they need no candle, neither the light of the sun, for the Lord God giveth that light, and they shall reign for ever and ever."

To return to St. Paul. Immediately after the expression of his wish to visit Spain, he adds this phrase: "But now I go unto Jerusalem." Unless we know the circumstances of his history, this may seem like a desire to escape reality, for to us Jerusalem, in its mystical sense, is a symbol of a castle in Spain. But it was far different to him; it was there that his enemies lived, who were thirsting for his life. He knew that it was the most dangerous spot in the world for him, and what happened proved that he was not mistaken. He went there, and it was the beginning of his imprisonment, and finally led to his death.

It is extraordinary how history repeats itself. London has for many years been the symbol of security and romantic history to millions of English-speaking people throughout the world. "As safe as the Bank of England," "As solid as St. Paul's," seemed the last word in security. But now, to visit London is not the easiest thing in the world, and when you get there you may find danger and privation; but the love and admiration of men who love freedom everywhere is given to that old city in a measure never known before. It may be that, in years to come, when men see the picture of these days in true perspective, in this bombed, weary and aging shrine of freedom they will see humanity's castle in Spain.

61

Sixty Years After

TWO OR THREE YEARS after Queen Victoria had been pro-
claimed Empress of India, at the beginning of the twilight
of one of the great ages of history, a wandering Bishop
sat in a birch-bark canoe on Lake Nipigon, one of the
most glorious and the least known of our Canadian
inland seas. It lies fifty miles north of Lake Superior and
is the authentic source of the great St. Lawrence waterway. It is probably the cradle of the Ojibway race, from
where the language and the legend of Hiawatha sprung.

As the canoe rested to let the paddlers gain their breath,
a flotilla of little craft came around the point. They were
searching for the Great Black Coat of whose arrival they
had heard. Munedoshans, the Chief, who bore the name
of the Son of the Great Spirit, told the Bishop that he
knew Hiawatha was dead and would never come back,
and he desired that a Black Coat should come and teach
them the religion of Christ.

In answer to an appeal in one of the London papers, a
young Irish clergyman came out to found a mission on
the distant shores of the lake. It was long before the
first transcontinental railway was built, and when the
guileless family of the young Irishman arrived at Prince
Arthur Landing they had to complete the journey by
sailboat and canoe. In the year 1881 the pilgrim pitched
his tent and built his altar in the wilderness. The missionary ideal burned bright in those days, and it seemed

perfectly natural that a man should go to the ends of the earth to proclaim salvation to the heathen.

In ten years great changes took place. The Canadian Pacific Railway had been completed, and many of the Indians came down to meet the challenge of civilization, but in the meantime the church had been erected and the last of the pagans had been baptized. Sometimes it is worth considering how much or how little modern civilization has blessed the aborigines in any land. Lake Nipigon was famous chiefly as the source of the Nipigon River, the Mecca of fishermen all over the world. For thirty miles its clear, crystal rushing waters tore in cataracts down to Lake Superior. The waters were so swift that none but trout could live there, and the "lesser breeds without the law" lived in the still lakes while the kings of the river reigned supreme. The first devil to come to this northern Eden was the commercial fisherman, with his tugs and his acres of nets to defile the lake. Later on two dams were built, one at the Virgin Falls, where the river begins, and the other at Camp Alexander. It was an improvement from the point of view of power development, and it was a help to the lumber companies, but alas, the river itself has lost many of its rapids, and the coarser fish have come to thrive in artificial lakes where they never could have lived before, and, like other aristocracies, the survivors among the speckled trout are deep down in their few remaining fastnesses, bombed by the mills of pulpwood to make Sunday edition for tired Christian business men.

This summer two surviving sons of the man who built the forgotten altar attempted to recapture youth and romance at the scene of their childhood. One came from California and one from Eastern Canada. They met

191

almost as strangers at Fort William. It took just three hours in a motor car to cover the distance which they used to travel in three weeks. The portages and canoes are only a memory, even to the Indians. A great motor boat with a Diesel engine crossed the lake in three hours, and there was the place of memory and dreams.

There were no more birch-bark canoes parked on the yellow sands, the moist coolness of which was still unforgotten. The church had been burnt down, the old log houses were gone, a modern mill had been erected where two ships a day attracted Indians from distant places to become white men and learn how to spend money, but not one of the old tribe was left except a boyhood comrade who by reversion was now known as the Old Chief. He had become fabulous to the newcomers, and enjoyed their deference and played up to his age. If he lives another five years he will think that he has reached their goal of 100 years.

But there was still some sign of the altar. When the Chief knew who the visitors were, he beckoned to them, and with surprising agility shuffled through a narrow path into the woods, and there he revealed his secret shrine. It was a perfectly kept graveyard. With the clairvoyance of genius the old man refused to compete with the lush underbrush, and each grave was covered with clean yellow sand from the beach. There were crosses, painted white, everywhere, and clean jam jars with the labels carefully washed off were wired to the arms of each cross, and these were filled with wild flowers from the woods. He was the last of the Mohicans, and as he played to Kitchemunedo he spoke of the life of man as a tale that is told by the camp fire, and asked that he might rejoin those that he had known and loved, in the eternal camping ground.

62

A Divided Personality

IT IS A REMARKABLE THING how the Bible seems to have anticipated some of the greatest and most widely publicized truths of modern psychology. In a simple narrative told by the least sophisticated of the Gospel writers, we have a picture of the Great Physician of the body and the soul landing from a boat on a desert shore. A ghastly figure rushes from one of the tombs on the hillside. He is almost naked; there are marks on his wrists from the fetters with which well-meaning friends have vainly tried to bind him. He is a poor half-mad creature, but when we learn his history we feel that he is our own brother. We are admitted to one of those characteristic clinics which Jesus loved. The first thing that He asked the patient was, "What is thy name?" There is more than sanity, there is something like inspired intuition in his answer, as he replied, "My name is legion"—that is to say, he was not one person but many. He was a battle ground. He was at war with himself. Every one knows that we meet such people not only in the psychopathic wards of our hospitals. We know some of them among our friends, and we sometimes meet them as we live with ourselves. There is an inner conflict in every man's life, but every one knows something of a divided personality. It may be said that this has nothing to do with religion, that it is the exclusive field of the psycho-analyst, but we are not so sure of this because the whole problem goes down to the deep, primordial areas of the soul. Some of our instincts are without moral sense. In the conscious mind there is a recognition of right and wrong, but our ideals are continually fighting against our lower selves. That is what Paul meant when he said: "O wretched man that I am! Who shall deliver me from the body of this death?" It is a cry of sheer agony.

It may be helpful to look at this classic case as a measure of our own lives. For this poor fellow was wretched. The story says: "Always, night and day, he was crying and cutting himself with stones." He was wounding himself; he was his own worst enemy. This is not an abstract theory. It is human experience. We notice also that this man was anti-social. He lived alone, probably because nobody could live with him. Because he fought with himself, he fought with everybody else. When we go to pieces, when we lose our tempers, when we stab right and left, we may call it nerves, but often the real reason is that we lack inner harmony, and therefore we can find no harmony in this gregarious world where men and women are not wrapped in cellophane, but gain their sorrows and their joys by contact with their kind.

We are not surprised that every one thought that this wild man was incurable. Nobody had any hope for him. He had no hope for himself. In the vivid Gospel phrase, "No man could tame him." Of course he is an extreme case, but, all the same, we recognize if we are honest with ourselves that we can learn something from him.

What can religion do with such a life? The first thing

194

that Jesus did was to make a hopeless man believe that he had something to live for. He gave him the germ of faith. Again, this tempest-tossed man found peace, for when we have peace with God we have peace within ourselves. Peace is not the absence of war. It is the presence of justice and joy, domestic or foreign. It is what men get when they have a life which deserves to survive. It is not what men get when they refuse to fight or when they have been so badly beaten they can fight no more; that is death. Perhaps the special legacy that Christ has given to every follower of His is, "Peace I leave with you, My peace I give unto you."

We close the case history of a man who is discharged, cured in body and mind, with the advice of Christ's parting words. He was sent back to the intimate circle of his own family. In his ecstatic joy at his deliverance, it is no wonder that he wanted to give up everything and follow the Master, but it was pointed out to him that the best thing that he could do was to go home and show how great things the Lord had done for him.

63

"The Candle of the Lord"

THE LITTLE VILLAGE OF MURRAY BAY, on the banks of the St. Lawrence, a hundred miles below Quebec, is one of the most beautiful and peaceful spots in Canada. Between the road and the great river which lies below, a fitting gateway to an Empire, there is a stone church erected by the summer residents which stands in a grove of trees. Last summer we looked at a lonely grave outside the church. There was a simple stone which commemorated a name well known in Canadian history and then this striking inscription taken from the Book of Proverbs, "The spirit of man is the candle of the Lord." It was late in the afternoon and the colors of the sunset were deepening; the hills were a dark purple and we thought of the story of man's pilgrimage to this New World. Somehow we could not forget the challenge of the cryptic epitaph. In very few places does man seem so unimportant as in a grove between the mountains and a great river. Surely God's candle ought to be something more majestic, for this is the land of the Northern Lights. Artists come here from Europe to paint an incredible sunrise, and in the late fall the stars themselves seem to hang like candelabra from the ceiling of the heavens. "Lord, what is man that Thou art mindful of him?" And yet, when you come to think of it, if it were not for man, all these beautiful things mean nothing at all. As far as we can see, the only spiritual candle to be found on this planet is the spirit of man.

The picture which the words suggest is very simple. An unlighted candle is standing in the darkness and some one comes to light it. You can strike fire from a match, but everything is vague and uncertain until the candle catches the flame. It burns straight and clear and constant. The candle is glorified by the fire, and the fire is revealed by the candle. Surely these two things were created for each other. If you try to light gunpowder, it only explodes. A piece of birchbark will give you fireworks for a few glorious minutes and then die in your hand; iron will glow a sullen red, but a candle gives its life in quiet light as long as it lives. When we think of these things we begin to get a new idea of the dignity of man. It does not seem so preposterous, after all, to think that this world is made for man, and that from man all things in the world get their true value and the verdict of their destiny.

We have been hearing much about the Torch of Freedom during the last week. It touches the imagination. It may be questioned whether a bomber is its ideal vehicle, but the humble candle has given light to men in darkness since the beginning of time.

First of all we notice in time of crisis how much depends on the leadership of one man. Surely the King and Queen have been the candles of the Lord to the British people during the last two years. It seems only yesterday that a young man stood straight and slim in a white silk shirt in Westminster Abbey to be crowned with all the age-long ceremonial of the mystic kingship of England. The whole service was a dedication, and since that time the light of the kingship has burned in a steady flame. The picture of the King and Queen appearing with magical regularity after all the great bombing of the cities of England has stirred the love and admiration of all our people. A Chicago newspaper not long ago published a little poem, "London Bridge Is Falling Down," which speaks of a Queen who did not forget to put on her gayest gown and stay in town "when London bridge was falling down." The face of Winston Churchill has been a candle in the darkness of the last year to the eyes of those who love faith and freedom.

Canadians are willing to admit that sometimes a nation can be a candle to the rest of the world. The English character may not suggest a volcano, but its serene and joyous light is leading the souls of men through the dark tunnel to the living world in the daylight which lies beyond.

64

The Blessedness of Work

DURING THIS WEEK thousands of people will bring their summer holidays to a close. The short and passionate Canadian summer seems to concentrate all thoughts of recreation in about two calendar months. To rest is sweet, but the sunburn soon wears off and we are confronted by the necessity of work.

Perhaps never in our time has it been so difficult to appreciate the spiritual quality of work as at the present hour. We are looking upon a world society which shows signs of disintegration. We believe that our Empire has been chosen for the difficult and conspicuous task of fighting almost single-handed for all the spiritual traditional values which seem to make life worth living for mankind. In other days, however monotonous a man's job might be, at least he felt that he was doing something to justify his existence in a world where there were hope, light, and the probability that faithful toil and prudence would secure for him a peaceful old age. But now, to many people, ordinary work seems futile, and it is easier sometimes to join the ranks of those who, wearing the King's uniform, have cast the world away and given themselves for the freedom of mankind.

But it is still necessary that the majority of people should carry on the unromantic labor which may yet win the war. And, therefore, it may not be inappropriate to point out the religious side of honest labor. There is a story told of Lord Palmerston, who once heard a sermon in which the preacher spoke some plain words about everyday religion. The Victorian statesman muttered as he left the church: "Things have come to a pretty pass when religion is allowed to interfere with a man's private life." And yet, surely, the right place for a man to express his Christianity is in his life between Monday morning and Saturday night. There was a time when men felt, if they did not say it, that one day belonged to God and the other days to the devil; that one book was God's Book, and that it did not matter whose spirit was in the daily papers; that as long as there was a church on every second corner in the city it guaranteed the respectability of the rest of the block, even if it was rather bad for real estate values. We are beginning to learn now that such hypocrisy is the reason why Christianity seems to have failed in so many departments of modern life. God claims all man's life. "Six days shalt thou labor and do all that thou hast to do." But when a man works for himself and lives for himself he exhausts himself, but when he works for others wisely and well he works for God also.

The early Christians understood the idea of the dignity of work. They did not tolerate the later conception of life, which implied that the man who preached and prayed was necessarily more holy than the one who labored for his bread with his own hands. Perhaps it was for this very reason that St. Paul was so careful not to be a charge on the early converts of the Church. There is no doubt that in these trying days honest, simple work brings a mystic peace to the soul that cannot be found in any other way.

The duty to work implies the right to work, and this brings a problem which cannot be dealt with here; but this much may be said: that one of the lessons of the present war which must never be forgotten is that if it is possible in our complex, modern world to find work for every man, even for destructive, if necessary purposes, when peace returns no statesman should ever say that it is impossible to find a place for the man who wants to work in days of peace.

Work and character are interrelated. In George Eliot's poem "Stradivarius," the great violin maker looks upon himself as God's messenger of music to the world. He is not at all certain that God Himself ever expects that the work shall be done without a human agent:

> 'Tis God gives skill, but not without men's hands,
> He could not make Antonio Stradivari's violins
> without Antonio.

In catastrophic times men and women will best prepare themselves for whatever God sends by doing their daily work. England, at the present moment, is a perfect example of how to live nobly in dangerous days.

65

Music

IT REQUIRES NO APOLOGY to write a religious article on the subject of music, for to multitudes of people music is not only an aid to religion, but it is religion itself. When we think of the millions of people who sit beside the radio and listen for three hours to one of the great symphonies, and know that the applause, louder and more prolonged than that to be heard at any hockey game, comes from the hearts of those who not only hear but see the great orchestra, it must be admitted that here is a force which goes deep down into man's primeval soul.

What a wonderful book is the Bible! It is the book of all beginnings. From the moment when the Divine Spirit "was present and, with mighty wings outspread dovelike, sat brooding on the vast abyss," we are carried through the morning mist of centuries to the cradle of all human institutions. Genesis gives us the first day on this planet. It tells of the first family, and in the fourth chapter it speaks of three pioneers of the human race. Tubal Cain, the first metal worker; Jabal, the first man who made a tent; and Jubal, "he was the father of all such as handle the harp and organ."

Who was this man who first gave music to the world— the first singer and the first organist? Here is one greater than Bach or Handel, Haydn or Mozart, Beethoven or Wagner, because he conceived the idea. Others developed it, but we owe the world of music to Jubal. He was probably a nomad who lived in the open air. Many a time he heard the wind whistling in the reeds by the river, Euphrates, and the twanging of the bowstring was melodious to his ear. The suggestion came to him from nature. The world was full of harps and organs. It must have been a later Israelite who discovered that there was music in a ram's horn.

Scientists tell us that there is music everywhere if our ears could only catch it. Harding King speaks of "the song of the sand," pointing out that morning and evening the contracting grains boom like Big Ben. Volumes have been written of the Memnon of Thebes, whose music at sunrise was a legend for centuries. In the furthest north on a clear winter night when the Aurora Borealis marches through the sky there is a sound like the swish of silken skirts. All lovers will agree with Shakespeare,

> There's not the smallest orb that thou beholdest,
> But in his motion like an angel sings.

Music is worship. The first and finest use of music was the offering of praise to God. Listen to the Psalmist, "O praise God in His holiness: praise Him in the firmament of His power. . . . Praise Him in the sound of the trumpet: praise Him upon the lute and harp." It is somewhat surprising to hear Martin Luther confess that music is the fairest and more glorious gift of God. He describes it as "discipline" because it makes people gentler, more moral and reasonable. A man may enter a church where a voluntary is being played, deformed, crippled, a hunchback, and, after hearing some of the divine music of Mendelssohn, he may walk down the street like a god.

> Such songs have power to quiet
> The restless pulse of care,

And come like the Benediction
Which follows after prayer.

And the night is filled with music,
And the cares which infest the day
Just fold their tents like the Arabs
And as silently steal away.

Music is inspiration. It has given new life and vision to multitudes. Music has made history. It has been one of the great forces of freedom, revolution and reform. Think of the "Marseillaise," which swept the French Provinces free from the invader a hundred and forty years ago. During the last Great War there was a song called "Tipperary," of which five million copies were sold in six months—a simple little thing with a touch of humor, love and hope. Only a few who sang it had ever seen the Rock of Cashel. It was crooned in the soft voice of negroes and shouted by lumberjacks of Northern Ontario. In every church music is of primary importance. Anthems may have their place, but the average man likes to think that he can sing, and it generally requires a tune that is associated with the precious memories of his life.

Some people have irreverently said that the reason why music is so popular is because it is one of those elemental things which go back to the days antecedent to human speech and reason, but it cannot be denied that here is one of the great comforting gifts which God gave to man when He gave him a soul, and, in days like these, when there is darkness over all the earth, songs in the night are a cordial for drooping spirits. It may be that with religion itself, because this thing is not bound by language, time or space, it will help to attune the human race to the Infinite.

66

The Four Vitamins

THERE IS A VERY SIMPLE and homely passage from the sayings of Jesus in the Sermon on the Mount which is full of suggestion for thoughtful people at the beginning of a year that may decide the future of Christian civilization.

We are all anxious about the future. We feel like praying and we would like to know what to pray for. We may well look to the Master for guidance.

Christ was talking about prayer. He was telling people how important it was, and how natural. God is our Father; and no normal father, if his son asked him for bread, would give him a stone. If the child asked for a fish, would he give him a snake? Or, instead of an egg, he would hardly torture him with a scorpion.

Now if the ordinary man with all his evil will give his best to his family, how much more shall our Heavenly Father give the Holy Spirit to them that ask Him?

There is a picture here from the childhood of the Saviour who was born in a manger. He was brought up in poverty. Nazareth is about twenty-five miles from the Lake of Galilee on the rocky spine of Palestine. The boys whose fathers fished in the lake seldom tasted meat. That was a luxury. But even the poorest family had a pair of millstones to grind the barley grain on the hills, and when the best fish had been shipped to the nobility in Jerusalem there would always be pickled herrings to give zest to the simple meal. No mother who had a roof over her head was without a few fowl, which lived on the scraps from the mill or the nets. Jesus must have known of many luxuries which He, like other children, often dreamed of. But He does not mention them here. They knew nothing of vitamins in those days, but that is what these simple articles of food were. The necessities of life. It is seldom noticed that our Lord, when speaking of the Spirit of God, assumes that it is not a luxury but necessary to spiritual survival.

When God wants to equip any human being for life's journey He gives His Spirit among the iron rations.

Our Empire is at war, and every effort is being rightly made to see to it that our people are properly fed. Never before has there been such preparation for production and transportation. The amount, the quality and the balance are scientifically calculated.

We say that we are fighting for spiritual values; but do we show this in our attitude toward Religion;

With all that is being done for our young men on active service, it should be taken for granted that a soldier has a soul and that he can appreciate spiritual reality just as much as any civilian.

In older days war was always followed by famine. We must beware that the famine of the soul does not overtake us. As we face this new year, let us remember that the lip service to Democracy and Christianity is not enough. At the risk of being misunderstood we assert that the greatest thing that could happen to the Empire is a new dedication to God. Let us not fear to confess to Him our many sins, and thank Him for that thin red line of spiritual idealism and sacrifice which is clearly discernible through our national history.

"Not by might, nor by power, but by My Spirit," saith the Lord of Hosts.

If Germany had only remembered the places where the greatest achievements of her history had been wrought!— Luther's bare cloister cell, Bach's humble abode, Kant's homely study, and Goethe's house, especially the simple workroom at the back.

But we must not forget that all our modern world has sinned against God. Our civilization has advanced far beyond the childlike mind of Jesus. For a generation or more our men of science have not been content until they have explained everything mechanically, and they think they have finished when they have done so, and yet warnings already begin to issue from strange sources. Man must believe in something divine, and understand that there is something of God in himself if he is to remain true to the purpose for which he was created.

67

The Fourth Commandment

THE SCHEME OF LIFE set forth in the Ten Commandments takes it for granted that God is supreme, and in order to emphasize this fact one nation was holy, one tribe was made the priestly caste, one building (the temple) was sacred, one part of the harvest (the first fruits) was dedicated, one day in seven was kept free as a religious festival—a symbol of God's claim upon the whole of man's being.

All the Commandments are founded on the necessity of man's nature and none more than this. There are many reasons which make it desirable that there should be a break in the world's business at least one day in seven. Physical health suffers and vigor of the body declines without it. As Lord Macaulay very truly said, "We are not poor, but richer, because we have through many ages rested from our labor one day in seven." The day is not lost. While industry is suspended, a process is going on quite as important to the wealth of nations as anything that is done on more busy days. For man is the greatest of all machines, and no mechanical unit would last for any time without it. He needs repairing and winding up so that he may return to his labor on Monday with a clearer mind and a livelier spirit. It is not conceivable that anything that makes a people healthier and wiser will ultimately make it poorer.

It is true that the thought of the old-fashioned Puritan Sunday gives a headache to the modern critic. We smile at the cold churches of the Puritans in which they sat through long services, with no fires in winter, but we sometimes forget that their spirits may have been warmed by an inner heat which even central heating cannot give to this degenerate age. We wonder what the Puritan would think if he came back to our world and saw thirty or forty thousand people sitting out in the open air on a bleak November day, their noses purple because of the icy wind and their teeth chattering from the cold, looking for two hours at a lot of college boys tumbling over one another on the frozen ground in frantic efforts to push a leather ball a few feet nearer to two poles at the end of field. It all depends on the point of view.

It is true that in the seventeenth century there were sermons two hours long, but even the most powerful preacher never went beyond twenty-five points, whereas an up-to-date Sunday newspaper aims at sixty-four.

We remember, many years ago, fishing on the Nipigon River with a great financier who came from Pittsburg. He had brought a whole flock of tents and servants into the wilds. It was before the days of radio and he had Indians in relays bringing him telegrams from the railroad station. The poor, simple Indians had been brought up to keep Sunday and he laughed at them and the young missionary as he spoke contemptuously of religion and all that it meant. He had a roll of bills in his fishing basket on the rock and, suddenly, there came to us the thought that there was no particular reason why he should live any longer. He was not ornamental or useful, and if it was not for the Ten Commandments we should most certainly have shoved him into the river. We have often thought since that many like him should be thankful that there are Ten Commandments in our modern life.

There is a determined effort in Canada to take the lid off Sunday, and this is not on the part of the people, but by certain interests which hate to see Sunday go to waste. Almost everything has been exploited but Sunday. Let the workingmen and young people beware of these men. Very often they are not thinking of liberty, but of dividends.

We are in favor of allowing almost every kind of Sunday recreation which is non-professional and non-money making. Certainly there is no reason why the rich man should be able to play his games on Sunday and the poor man be prevented. But let us draw a black line between these things and the aim to buy and sell and exploit the people for gain. God honors those who honor Him. There is wisdom as well as religion in the old words, "Remember the Sabbath day to keep it holy."

68

The Second Half of Religion

THE OTHER DAY WE SAW a fragment of a poem in blank verse entitled "Ultimatum Expires Midnight." We have not been able to find the name of the author and we shall not attempt to quote it, but the story is a parable which makes us think.

The time and scene are plainly contemporary. A deputation appears before heaven's gates to interview the Almighty. It is a very mixed grill—two mothers, a labor leader, an archbishop, a poet, who have apparently met on the way without any time to rehearse their petition. When the Father gently asked them what they wanted they only said: "Life is not worth living. Good Lord, deliver us."

"I must ask you two questions first," said the Creator. "Why do you not go to the Prince of Peace?" The answer was: "Because we're not sure that He can really help us now."

"Again," said the King of Kings, "I must ask what it is that you are afraid of."

They all began to speak independently. "It's this war. It kills women; it kills children, and leaves innocent people lying in cold rows on the pavement. Make us helpless children again. Take the skill from our fingers and the fire from our mind."

"Do you know what you are asking?" said God. "Do you want Me to uncreate you? I made you out of love; I made you for love; My Spirit is in you. Your beautiful world supplies you with everything that you need. Even now you have only half discovered the treasures which are hidden for you to find.

"It's up to you!"

Yes, it is up to us. The trouble with the world is that men and nations have not discovered how to get on together. Man knows far too much about the world outside and far too little about the mystery that lies within his soul.

Have we ever considered what it would mean if every individual lived on a planet of his own, swirling in icy coldness through space, thinking his own thoughts? Man under such conditions could not even love God, much less his neighbor. And yet our neighbors are worth knowing.

A Sunday school teacher was once trying to explain the Collect, which speaks of "the ministers and stewards of God's mysteries." The boys told him quite truly that the ministers and stewards were the clergy or teachers or anybody else doing His work, but when they were asked, "What are God's mysteries?" an inspired urchin put up his hand and answered, "Please, sir, we are." Yes, we are the mystery of all creation.

The second half of religion is that man should understand his neighbor and love him as himself. In His memorable interview with the young lawyer Jesus made this very plain as He introduced one of the most famous of His parables.

If men and nations could only understand their neighbors! Perhaps the chief difficulty about these neighbors of ours is that we cannot choose them. They come and go at random, and yet on our relationship and under-standing of them depends the future of the human race in this world.

There were many reasons why that lone Samaritan should not stop on the Jericho road. He was a foreigner; it wasn't his business, but pity got the better of him, and so caution and prejudices were forgotten. If he had been sensible there would have been no story. He *did* something.

It is strange that Jesus Christ, about Whom so much theology has been written, insisted that religion must be practical. Negative morality is colorless and unattractive.

Dr. Charles R. Brown of Yale, in an unforgettable sermon on this parable, suggests that the Syrian donkey on which the Samaritan rode, in modern life might be described in terms of a popular cheap car. Most of us can give a lift, if not to the hitchhiker, at least to the poor wounded brother who lies by the highway.

We all agree that man should love God with all his heart, but it may well be doubted whether the first part of religion is possible without the second.

69

The Ivory Gates

IT IS HARD TO HAVE ANY INNER LIFE these days. The whole
world is living under calcium lights which penetrate, not
only through the walls of our houses, but into the secret
recesses of the soul. It is a far cry to the Syrian desert
where the lonely watcher could sing to himself, "The
Lord is my Shepherd."

Many years ago an anxious Bishop suggested to the
Rector of a village church in England that he should have
a Quiet Day, and the answer was, "My Lord, we have
Quiet Days all the time. What we need is an Earthquake."

We can well remember in Hudson's Bay forty years
ago when Queen Victoria died, that no one in that
country knew anything about it until six months afterwards. On the whole, mankind does not desire a
sanctuary in days of continuous sunshine, but there are
times when the spirit cries for some refuge. Especially
when evil seems to be triumphant in the world, the
Christian is tempted to climb some Ivory Tower where
he may be far away from the discordant clamor of strife
and war. But this attitude of mind, while perfectly
natural, is bad for the world, and it is particularly bad
for the individual. No Ivory Tower for the Pilgrim, for
he has a march to make, but, nevertheless, our Heavenly
Father, who knows the necessities of human nature, has

provided Gardens of Refuge along the trail which leads to man's desire. There are Ivory Gates where the Pilgrim may enter to rest. These Gardens of the Soul are many. They are different in character, but each one performs a service of its own. We will mention only three.

The first is the nearest, within the reach of every one. One Refuge in time of trouble and anxiety is to seek the good and simple things which lie at the heart of normal human life. We can thank God that there are blessings without which our race would never have survived. From the days of the cave man, through the dark Middle Ages, there have always been elements which have made life worth living, and they protect us even today from the mass manias around us.

In time of war we ought to appreciate the ties of affection for our families and our friends. We can rejoice in that charmed circle within which the hearthfire glows, where neither fear nor hate can penetrate. We can see now with clearer eyes than ever before the beauty and meaning of kindly faces, and the magic of the common tasks of plain people who go to their work in the morning and return to their wives and children as the sun goes down.

Think of our glorious Canadian autumn! The drone of the aeroplane, without any fear of bombs, and the smell of the burning rubbish as the farmer clears his field for next spring's plowing.

The second Gate is called "Action." It may seem to contradict the spirit of this meditation, but every one knows the restfulness of work. Let us admit that the skies of the world are dark today. We all feel the moral mystery of life's spiritually overcast days. Thomas a Kempis, whose "Imitation of Christ" has passed into more than three thousand editions and has been translated into nearly every language, has this to say of his own seasons of "dryness, barrenness, unreality, emptiness: "At such times it is expedient for thee to flee to humble and outward works—Refresh thyself with good actions—Bear patiently thy dryness of mind, till I shall again visit thee." He knew, although he was a Saint, that feeling could not be commanded, but there was still work to do.

God said to Moses, by the shores of the Red Sea, "Why criest thou unto me? Speak to the children of Israel that they go forward." It is a relief to work. Sorrow may take from life its delights, but it can never take its duties. Work here, rest elsewhere, for the day is short and there is much to be done. The best way to put in your time this winter is to help your city, your country, and your God. For human hands are the only hands God can use.

The third Gate leads to the Garden of Hope, which is filled with the flowers and fragrance of the promise of God.

One day, when St. Francis was laying before God his troubles, the answer came to him, "Poor little man, why dost thou trouble thyself? I, Who made thee the shepherd of My order, knowest thou not that I am its Protector? If those I have called upon go, I will put others in their place, and if none existed, I would cause them to be born."

If the men who are to save the world and bring in the Kingdom of God are not alive, God will cause them to be born. And so, although we may not climb the Ivory Tower of Isolation, for we are Pilgrims, let us gird our loins with a good heart, believing that the trail will lead us to that one far-off Divine event to which the whole creation moves.

70

"I Go Afishing"

THESE WORDS ARE CHARACTERISTIC of one of the most lovable men in the whole gallery of the portraits of the Bible. He had the priceless gift of personality. We knew him better than any of his companions. Peter is always the centre of interest in any company. He was a fisherman, and whenever he embarked with his crew he always took the helm. Every word he says gives us a picture of a daring, impetuous sailor. He does not hesitate to argue with his Master. We remember his great confession, his prayer when he was sinking in the sea, his lusty affirmation of loyalty to Christ, his oaths of denial and the tears of his broken heart. It is a beautiful touch when, after the Resurrection, the Disciples were wearying for Christ. They wondered whether the news on Easter Day had been only a dream, but there was one man who knew what to do. When he was tired out, disillusioned and depressed Simon Peter said in effect: "I wish Jesus would come, but, in the meantime, I must do something. I go afishing."

Perhaps the Anglers' Club in self-defense is justified in pointing out that when the Founder of Christianity chose twelve Disciples He did not pick lawyers or parsons. The one business man was not a success, but the great majority of the crew were fishermen. There is something about the philosophy of fishing which appeals to men if it does not to women. Perhaps it is an excuse for doing nothing. It is a strenuous exercise, with long periods of inaction which may be used for meditation. Like all sailors, the average fisherman is an honest, simple soul who would rather be cheated than take advantage of another.

> *A feller isn't plotting schemes,*
> *   Out fishin';*
> *He's only busy with his dreams,*
> *   Out fishin';*
> *His livery is a coat of tan,*
> *His creed—to do the best he can;*
> *A feller's always mostly man,*
> *   Out fishin'!*

In the early days of the Christian Church, when the Disciples in the Catacombs of Rome were a secret society, the emblem of a fish was used as a Christian symbol. In many places you can still see a crude drawing of an unmistakable fish on the stones. The Greek word for a fish is "ichthus," and the first two letters, "I" and "Ch," which is one letter in Greek, reminded the initiated of Jesus Christ. Many of the early fathers spoke of Our Saviour as the great Fisher of men. You remember Our Lord's words to Peter when He told him to scrap his nets: "Fear not; from henceforth thou shalt catch men."

Many years ago a young Canadian missionary had the opportunity of preaching on deputation in England for a whole winter, and it fell to his lot to visit Yarmouth, the largest parish church in the world. It was the occasion of the Blessing of the Nets. The great fishing fleet which used to travel around the coasts of Britain had just arrived for the fall fishing. The streets were filled with men in sou'westers and girls in rubber boots who knitted as they walked. On Sunday a great seine net was draped around the walls. After the service the vicar, on speaking to the head of one of the companies, presented the missionary with the net for Hudson's Bay. He rather indicated that the fishermen were superstitious and were reluctant to use the net again. The next fall, at Albany, just before the ice came, all the old men who were too infirm to go to the hunting ground and a great company of widows and young women manned the net and set forth to catch their winter fish. They were small white fish, very like those in the Lake of Galilee in the days of Simon Peter. The net was carried out from the shore in the boat and paid out in a semicircle nearly two hundred yards in length. Three casts were made and hardly anything caught. It was nearly sunrise. In desperation the net was again let down, and this time it enclosed a whole school of fish. The net was filled with a churning mass which required extra help to draw it to shore. The fish were jumping out of the water, and suddenly a diabolical form appeared. It was a huge seal who had pursued his quarry to his own destruction. He was shot by the missionary, and a wise old Indian said: "Wouldn't it be wonderful if the Church's net could always catch not only sinners, but the devil too?" Unfortunately it has not yet been done. In that one haul the husky dogs and the poor of Albany had their food for the winter. It took half a day to carry the baskets to the yard, where they froze without artificial refrigeration.

There are many spiritual lessons to be learned from fishing which the parsons and people of the churches might well remember. For instance, Our Lord gave a word of advice that could only have come from a master fisherman: "Cast on the right side of the ship and ye shall find." Many overanxious sportsmen waste their strength and their bait in the wrong places. There are some dead pools where you will never get a rise. We learn again that we should never be afraid to change our methods. The silver king may be deadly one morning, while a brown hackle will do the trick under certain circumstances. The most depressing sight in the world is the picture of a man with a pipe in his mouth, seated on a dock with a long pole and a bait, hoping for hours for what he knows will never come.

In St. Luke's version of the story of the miraculous draught of fishes there is a significant sentence. When the Disciples were struggling with their great haul and the net was breaking, they beckoned to their partners to come to their help. There was good teamwork, sportsmanship and common sense. In days like these, when Christianity is fighting for its life, those who fish for the souls of men should have the courage and generosity to work together.

Finally, in this month of holidays, after such a year of anxiety that our generation has never known, when you are blue, when nothing seems to happen, when even the little worries of life are magnified, think of the sublime wisdom of an honest, distracted, faithful Christian: "I go afishing."

71

The Wings of the Morning

IT HAS TAKEN MAN A LONG TIME to conquer the material handicap of his body. He can think in terms of the universe, but even Nurmi could not run a mile in four minutes, and the average man cannot swim a mile in an hour. Still, man has striven through the ages to make his body catch up with his mind. This restlessness of the pushful civilized man is a trial to primitive people who do not like to hurry.

A certain Missionary Bishop was notorious for driving his canoemen on his long journeys. They could see no sense in it. On one occasion the Indians struck. They had paddled for ten days from daybreak to dark. But this morning they refused to strike their tents. When asked why, they said: "Our souls are three days behind us; we stay here till they catch up."

In La Guardia Field, twenty miles from New York, is one of the greatest and newest airports in the world. It is already overcrowded. In the rotunda there is a striking series of cartoons illustrating man's progress in the mastery of the world's greatest divider of mankind—the ocean. These heroic figures are historical and symbolic. First comes Noah with a dove on his wrist and his patient wife with an expression of relief on her face for a happy landing. The Ark is seen in the distance marooned on a cliff.

Then the Phoenician marines with an altar on the prow of a little ship as they set sail, after sacrificing to their gods, for a dash from one point to another on the Mediterranean.

Later the nautical and mathematical instruments of Greek scientists, and beyond the legend of Icarus, whose wings have become unstuck, diving headlong in the deep.

And so it went till the last century, when the captain of a South Atlantic liner pauses to wonder at the grace of an albatross which so easily passes him in flight.

The final picture shows Charles and Anne Lindbergh, young and vital, looking back on the ocean. Probably no nation should erect a monument to a hero till he is dead, but no man could crave a greater honor than to be chosen as a symbol of what many have by their lives and deaths made possible.

The Yankee Clipper is not beautiful at rest. She is like a monstrous duck decoy poised for flight upon the water. Her wings have a spread of 150 feet. There is room inside for more than sixty passengers. She flies from New York to Lisbon, nearly 4,000 miles, with never more than two stops, one at Bermuda and at the Azores.

With all the labor, science and care admitted, this ocean flight is a spiritual thing. It is a symbol of the immortality of man. There is something like death in the takeoff. The poor creature threshes the water trying to rise. . . . Up the Hudson to the George Washington Bridge, and then at the right moment mortality fades away and she rises like a bird for a flight that no eagle has ever known. The death rattle changes into the regular breathing of the four propellers in the upper air. . . .

In a few minutes we are above the clouds. In an hour we are in another world. Beneath is a floor of pure white mountains towering to fantastic peaks. The whole scene is like the Ice Age of the world. For the first time the sun sets in splendor far below; we share the view of God as He looks at the end of a day.

You cannot help thinking how the struggles and evils of life are settled in the higher levels of life. It is amazing that man as an engineer has discovered this truth while he will fight to the death in the primordial depths of his nature. We admit that there is danger in the intoxication of such a moment.

John Buchan, in his exquisite autobiography "Memory Hold the Door," describes his last meeting with his friend Lawrence of Arabia. He thought he had never looked so well, but on speaking to his wife, Lady Tweedsmuir said: "No, the man looks on the world as if he were God, and no man can do that and live." In ten days he was dead.

In four hours the ship began to descend, going through the clouds. She rocked like a canoe in the rapids. There below were the lights of Bermuda—we were in a different climate in five hours.

There is a great lesson in faith in the theory of blind flying. The greatest natural flier who ever lived cannot do by native wit what a young graduate can do with instruments and radio. Think of unerringly finding the little bay at Horta in the Azores after a night in the stratosphere. . . . But faith is balanced with judgment and common sense.

We left Bermuda at one hour after midnight and went to bed. Awakening at seven in the morning, we found that we had turned back just halfway because the landing at the Azores was reported unsafe from heavy swells. Two thousand miles for nothing except safety and the reputation of the company.

The following afternoon we went through to the Azores, dropping through the clouds like an arrow into a target. After two hours we were away again, and at sunset were gliding down the river at Lisbon, a thousand miles away. What an age we live in! Man, the Creator and the Destroyer. . . . Perhaps we should wait a while to let our souls overtake us.

"Such knowledge is too wonderful and excellent for me: I cannot attain unto it.

"Whither shall I go then from Thy Spirit: or whither shall I go from Thy Presence? If I climb up into heaven, Thou are there: if I go down to hell, Thou art there also.

"If I take the wings of the morning: and remain in the uttermost parts of the sea;

"Even there also shall Thy hand lead me: and Thy right hand shall hold me."

72

Canada Through the Telescope

EVERY CANADIAN who loves his country should some time go away, the further the better, and look at this Dominion through the telescope of the imagination till he can feel the romance of its story and catch the vision of its destiny.

The greatest advantage of flying to Europe is not the saving of time, but the new perspective gained. As the plane glides down through the clouds after four thousand miles of ocean and a thousand miles of European coast line, you look at a map and see a postage stamp called the British Isles. You ask whether this is the place which has stirred humanity for so many hundred years. It is the heart of an Empire whose members are far away, and the salt sea highways are the veins where its life blood flows.

It is true that other little countries have moulded mankind. Palestine gave us something without which life would not be worth much, and the lamp of mind which Greece lighted in her brief hour still shines. But England is different. She first taught men how to be disciplined and free. When the New World was discovered, she was a late starter in the race. All the lands of glamour and gold were already taken. The adventurers of England had to take the Northern way. In the providence of history they came to a land of pine, spruce and prairie and snow. They dug in; they lived and died. The children grew strong, away from the centre of the world's life. They pushed their way to the Pacific Ocean, and after 200 years they presented Victoria with half a continent. There were many in the Old Country who thought we should set up housekeeping for ourselves on a modest scale. . . . For the past fifty years we have built railways, capital cities and equipment for a population of thirty millions. After the last war, during the period of disillusionment, it became apparent that the growing of No. 1 hard wheat, the wholesale cutting of our forests and the excavation of the Pre-Cambrian shield was not enough to build a nation. We needed population.

In some strange way England refuses to grow old. John Bull believed in bleeding himself of men and money, which is probably the reason why he has never had a stroke. Three years ago the Specialists said that the end was near, but the Battle of Britain has shown that the land of Shakespeare and Nelson is still sound to the core. The people are tired, but they will never surrender.

One must think of what England will be after the war. The miracle of that workshop of the world can hardly be repeated. It will no longer be a place of cheap labor. All her investments of two centuries at home and abroad have been thrown into the melting pot with sacrificial joy. She will be proud but poor to begin life again.

It was here that I looked at Canada through the glass. There appeared the providence of her history: her place in the centre of the oceans, with front doors East and West; the wide open spaces calling for people: her unlimited source of electric power guaranteed by her rivers: her natural resources. I could not help dreaming of the coast of Nova Scotia as a second Clyde bank and picturing the great waterway from Belle Isle to Fort William lined for 2,000 miles with yards and factories for world trade.

Unless the millennium comes there will always be an air force, and the air training scheme should be a permanent institution for war and peace.

Canada must decide. One thing is clear: She cannot remain forever as she is now. She is too big and the time has come for a decision, whether gradually to develop the Western Hemisphere complex or boldly to take her place as the keystone of the British Empire. It does not need a prophet or a son of a prophet to foretell that when this war is over there will be the greatest opportunity that Canada has ever known to bring those of our own blood to a land which needs them as much as they need us. The old fear of pioneering will have gone. Money has come to mean nothing in the Mother Country—space, freedom, security for children are vital.

Canada for a moment glowed with a mystic light.

It may well be that the attitude of our Government and people to this challenge will decide the future of the British Empire. "Who knoweth whether thou be come to the kingdom for such a time as this."

The Invisible City

THE QUESTION IS SOMETIMES ASKED, "Which is the greatest city in Canada?" Some might say Montreal, with its long and romantic story, its great cosmopolitan population and its site on the St. Lawrence. Others may prefer Toronto, with its British traditions and its modern progress. Many who have seen Vancouver, with her forest sentinels and mountain ramparts and the Pacific binding her to the Orient, feel that she is a City of Destiny.

But today our hearts turn to another. It is far away. It has no name, but its mystic spires can be seen more clearly than the Arches of Amiens or the Belfroi of Mons. Its silent streets are scattered all over France and Belgium. The two marble pylons and a figure of Canada, like Rachel weeping for her children, is its shrine.

It is a Canadian City. Separated from Canada by 2,000 miles of ocean, neither time nor space can ever alter its character. Some day we may change, but every summer as long as history is written the breeze that blows over the poppies will be perfumed with the memory of Canada at her best. Not only the Vimy acres deeded by the French Government, but on the Somme, in the Ypres Salient, on the sand dunes of Etaples, are fields that will be forever Canada.

It is a City of Youth. Most of the 60,000 who gave their

lives were in their twenties. The very flower of our manhood—with all the devil-my-care humor and practical sanity of a free people, they tackled the ugly job of war in the same way that they built the Canadian railways or prospected Cobalt. We have missed that Lost Battalion sorely. Those who would have been our business leaders, our pathfinders and statesmen went, leaving a dangerous gap between their disillusioned fathers and mothers and a new generation of boys and girls, born or going to school in a decade when old cables are parting and ancient lights dimmed forever.

But their youth has made their country forever young.

It is a City of Faith. They never said much about it, but they believed in Canada's star. They had nothing to do with the causes of the war. They were not even consulted, but, when they were needed, they gave all they had. They hated war like hell.

The instinct for memorials is as old as man. There is no diviner thing in the human mind than the power to escape out of the world of the material into the realm of the ideal, peopled as it is by the brave hearted. "The spirit of man is the candle of the Lord." And so, however great Canada may become, however practical, amid problems very different from war days, she will never forget the spirit of her sons who once crossed the Atlantic Ocean to die for her. We could do with 60,000 young Canadians of like spirit in these days of depression. Perhaps they are with us still. In the words of Pericles the Great Athenian: "Heroes have the whole earth for their tomb. Their bodies are buried in the earth from which they came, but their souls live on in other lands and in other years, woven into the stuff of other men's lives.

74

"Known to God"

BY SOME STRANGE COINCIDENCE of fate November seems to
have become the month of memorials. As if it were not
enough that the leaves should be blown by the north wind
to make a wonderful carpet for our Canadian land, and
let a little more light through the sombre tracery of the
bare branches, the days are haunted by red-letter Saints,
black-letter Saints and khaki Saints. The months begins
with All Saints' Day; All Souls' Day follows, and last
week the great modern festival of the Armistice Remembrance tells us that love is stronger than death. Man's
spirit is so susceptible to the influence of the ideal that it is
possible to escape for a time from the stark reality of
existence.

It may seem to be an anticlimax to the festivals that
have just passed to speak for a moment about the strange
impartial way of God in dealing with some of the greatest
and most beloved of His sons. Not all heroes are buried
in the Pantheon. It is the life of a man that counts, and
not his death. How shall we think of the unknown graves
in a foreign land today? Those lonely mounds which
mark the resting-place of heroic men who have been laid
to sleep in silent glory. Men and women, too, who loved
much and gave much and to whom much shall be
forgiven, who saw a Promised Land, but never set foot
upon its peaceful soil.

There are some graves, of course, that we can find. There is that field in lonely Seyros where lies Rupert Brooke, who sang his own requiem before he passed out of sight:

> "If I should die, think only this of me,
>   That there's some corner of a foreign field
>   That is forever England."

Some leave no trace of their passing. There is no shrine, no sacred spot upon which a pilgrim can build an altar, but somehow there is a universal message in their anonymous end. These unknown graves mark the unfulfilled purposes in life. They are eloquent of the temple locked in the heart which has never been permitted to be built on the earth. These men, like the seer of old, saw beyond the world and died to conquer in the power of the Unseen. They saw the shining towers of the City of God far away on the horizon, but they perished by the wayside and never arrived. The light lured them on and then left them.

This is how the dull eyes of the world regard the end of the men of faith; but, truly speaking, the world's pioneers of the spirit die with their music in them. They hold converse with God and they share His secret, and when they die God buries them with His secret in their heart. We can hide nothing from Christ, and the poetry of the death of Moses is part of all life. God buried him; his grave was never known. Somewhere on Nebo's lonely mountain, under the dark pines, with the stars for tapers tall, God's own hand in that desert land put him to sleep.

Yes, there is a paradox in the end of the world's greatest men. Think of Socrates, the purest teacher of morality that the ancient world knew, drinking the hemlock in his prison cell while his judges went free under the groves of ancient Athens.

John Wycliffe, the man who gave the English Bible to his countrymen, his tomb in Lutterworth desecrated, the ashes cast into the Wye, thence to the Severn, and finally carried, like the influence of his teaching, to the wide ocean of the world.

Oliver Cromwell, with all due deference to Maurice Colbourne, who taught kings that they had a lith in their necks, disturbed in his resting-place by the courtiers of Charles II, who held in his pocket the golden louis of his French masters.

And, last of all, Jesus, an obscure Galilean peasant, in a little Province of Rome, was unknown in the centre of the world's life. The Eternal City knew nothing of the life and death of Jesus of Nazareth until the messengers of the Cross told the redeeming story years later. It could have been truly said by a newspaper reporter in the days of Pontius Pilate that the Galilean Prophet arrived in Jerusalem and was arrested as a dangerous traitor, tried by the religious and civil powers on the same day, and executed with two other criminals outside the city walls. The soldiers saw Him safely buried before sundown, and Caiaphas slept the night sure that the story was ended. All of which reminds us that no life is finished until God has written the epitaph.

75

Advent

THE CALENDAR OF THE CHRISTIAN YEAR begins next Sunday. It may seem that, since the birth of Christ is the mountain peak of human history, there is no need for any introduction, but for many centuries it has been the custom of the Christian Church to set aside the four weeks before the Nativity as a period of preparation. The word "advent," of course, means the coming of the One who has changed the spiritual viewpoint of mankind. At first sight it seems remarkable that traditionally the Advent season has been looked upon in the light of the Judgment, while Christmas is the joyous festival of Divine love.

It must be admitted that in recent times most Christians have neglected the old lesson of the Advent. In happier days in Victorian England the Sunday before Advent was popularly called "Stir-Up" Sunday, because the Collect begins with the words "Stir up, we beseech Thee, O Lord, the wills of Thy faithful people." The average English housewife was reminded that it was time to stir the ingredients for the Christmas pudding. For two or three generations our forefathers lived through a period of invincible optimism, and it was perhaps natural that the sombre side of human history should be conveniently ignored. But through many of the earlier centuries this was not the case. In some of the finest cathedrals of the

233

Norman period in England when you go up into the choir you will notice the black oak stalls where the ends have been bored to hold tallow candles, where the monks of old in the days when the world was very evil and the times seemed waxing late used to night after night in the dark December days sing the Dies Irae of the Advent season. This most terrible and famous of all the hymns of the Church is supposed to have been written in the thirteenth century by Thomas of Celano. Goethe used it in "Faust." Sir Walter Scott, who quoted it on his death-bed, has translated some verses in "The Lay of the Last Minstrel."

> *Oh! on that day, that wrathful day,*
> *When man to judgment wakes from clay,*
> *Be Thou the trembling sinner's stay,*
> *Though heaven and earth shall pass away!*

The germ of this hymn may be found in the Book of the Revelation of St. John: "Lo, He cometh with clouds, and every eye shall see Him." As we approach the Christmas season in this year of grace 1940 we are conscious of the fact that the coming of Christ is, in a sense, a judgment for the souls of men. It is perfectly true that He came as a Saviour and as a Light in the darkness, but, nevertheless, His very presence in modern life is a judgment.

We all have our standards in personal life. There is something by which we measure everything that we do. In literature, art, business and amusements this is profoundly true. Jesus Christ is the standard of character, and perhaps nowhere is that more apparent than in the international scene where nations strive. Our national life is judged by Him whose clear and searching eyes reveal the inmost thoughts of men. Yes, set Jesus in any place, He cannot help judging. He sifts and separates men. If we believe that the Saviour of the world is in any sense actually among us today, it is not necessary that we should ask to hear Him speak as He looks down upon our so-called Christian civilization. We are reminded of the time when He stood before Pilate and answered him never a word. But, all the same, it was not Jesus that was being judged; it was Pilate who was in the dock, and his own conscience did not let him forget that fact.

Some years ago a party of tourists were doing the art galleries of Florence, where in the marble palaces there hang some of the greatest paintings in all the world. It was a hot day and there was one man who had been reluctantly dragged into the procession by his wife. In self-defense he thought it necessary to criticize everything that he saw. "I don't think much of this" was repeated so often that the long-suffering curator at last said: "Sir, these works of art are not judged by the visitors. They judge those who are privileged to look upon them."

Christmas marks the day when the Son of God became man, and when He visited us He decided to remain. He is still here. His presence makes it necessary for those who love good to turn to Him, and for those whose choice is evil to hate the One who reveals them for what they are.

76

The Last Enemy

THE DAY BEFORE YESTERDAY was observed by the whole English-speaking world, and probably in some degree among most of the civilized races of mankind, as a great Religious Festival. We use these words deliberately because when one looks into the history of the ideal of Remembrance Day, which sprang into being after the great Armistice of 1918, it is apparent that there is a mystical and spiritual quality hidden here which is of the very essence of religion. The fact that the commemoration was largely observed in religious buildings and on a distinctly religious day confirms this conclusion.

It is a strange thing how man's heart is sometimes a truer guide than his intellect. Ten years ago it was suggested that logically there was no reason why we should continue to hold special services for a dead war indefinitely. We see now that our emotional instinct was right, for this day is a Festival of Death.

All men and women fear death. This is an instinct which is as old as human life. It belongs to youth and to age and is found among every race of mankind. It is true, no doubt, that war has brought this hidden fear to the forefront of our minds, but even in ordinary times in many ways we have tried to think and speak of death in terms which gild its real quality. The very fact that not only in the Bible but among the North American Indians the convention in speaking of one who is deceased that "he is not" is significant. We are all searching our hearts these days to find the hidden springs of life. The great word "freedom" must first be won in every individual heart, and it is worth while to analyze the terror which is our universal enemy.

First of all it should be admitted that there is such a thing as a healthy instinct of self-preservation which is kept alive by the dread of death. If men do not fear death, suicide would be very common, but Some One has hedged the gate of life in shadows so that none should carelessly try to pass.

"The sting of death"—that phrase used by St. Paul in the great chapter read at most Christian funerals—has two other elements than the one which he mentions. Probably the first is associated with the physical act of dying. This is a very real dread to some people. We all know what pain is, and somehow or other we feel that if pain is so hard to bear death itself must be worse. No one can hope to avoid death. Sooner or later it comes to us all. Dust returns to the earth as it was, and the spirit goes to the God who gave it. But we are mercifully assured that "the agony of death" is felt much more by those who watch than by the one who is passing away to the land where there is no pain. Sir Frederick Treves, the great English surgeon, says: "The last moments of life are more distressing to witness than to endure. The closing moments of it are, as a rule, free from suffering." Besides this, it has often been observed that, after a long illness, there comes a sense of detachment to the sufferer as if the things of earth, the joy and pain of mortal existence, were not important any more. Merely from the physical point of view it is true that man may say to death, "You are only a shadow."

The second element in "the sting of death" is mental—the thought that it is the end of our hopes, our loves, our ideals and our strivings. It is solemn indeed to feel that one can cease to be. Now it is here that Christ comes into His own. The most blessed thing in Christianity is the assurance that death is not the end. To the man who has the Christian faith in his heart, no longer is death that "undiscovered country from whose bourn no traveller returns." There was One who did return, and He said "Peace I leave with you, My peace I give unto you. . . . . Let not your heart be troubled, neither let it be afraid."

The third element in "the sting of death" is judgment. St. Paul, whose words we have quoted, said: "The sting of death is sin; and the strength of sin is the law." The meaning of these words must be that man's divinest gift is a conscience, and that his conscience may make him fear to stand before his Maker who knows everything about him. It is probably true that this thought is not as universal as it was in an earlier age. People who grew up in the days when the punishments of God were luridly preached felt the seriousness of judgment more than those who, in modern days, have been taught that God is an Indulgent Parent. But no one has a right to make light of conscience. It finds support in the law of cause and effect, which runs through all creation. The meaning of Christianity is most clearly seen in its power to release man from this last fear. He who is the incarnation of God, the Picture of all that is beautiful and pure in perfect life, tells us that man is the child of God and that His mercy endureth forever; that the many mansions of the Creator, whether here or beyond, are only different rooms in the House of Infinite Love.

77

Indian Christmas

WE REGRET TO SAY that we are late in reminding our readers that Christmas is coming. It may be due to the infirmity of age, but we seem to be getting later every year. The world is more up to date than the Church. Santa Claus is the Cleopatra of modern business, "age cannot wither nor custom stale" his infinite variety. A writer in the Southern Churchman last week tells us how his city government had already arranged a Christmas tree on Nov. 26 to launch the Christmas season. The streets were lined with trees from Maine decorated with colored lights. Carols were blared from loudspeakers. It has come to pass that no modern little town of Bethlehem can ever be still and silent any more, and the brass band is our substitute for the angels' song.

Many years ago, before the days of airplanes and radios, the Christmas season came to the little town of Albany on James Bay. There was a settlement at the mouth of the greatest northern river in Ontario. There were only three mails a year. One was brought through Hudson Strait from Scotland in August on the sailing ship which carried all the supplies from the outside world. A canoe made a round trip of a thousand miles in June and September. It was the twilight of the 250-year reign of the Hudson's Bay Company. There was a white church in the village. The Indians lived in birch-bark wigwams.

The company's fort was like a feudal castle dominating the scene.

It was the hunting season; most of the families were far away. Two days before the Birth of Christ, a missionary standing on the bank saw something like a black serpent winding its way down the slope a mile away. It was a Cree family on the march. The man, breaking a trail on snowshoes, led the way; behind came his wife with a baby on her back. There were four starved dogs hauling a toboggan. Two or three half-grown children brought up the rear. They settled down in half an hour, after travelling three days through the woods at 30 degrees below zero. One thing brought them: Like the magi of old, they came to see a sign.

By Christmas Eve there were a hundred tents around the church. In the meantime the interior was transformed. A cedar tree was nailed to the end of each pew, a silver star made from a new tin plate hung on a wire, incredible flowers were fashioned by deft hands from colored paper so that the aisle looked like the Celestial City. The floors were scrubbed; the box stove shone like black marble.

On Christmas morning (while it was yet dark) the church was filled—the men on one side, the women on the other. Every man wore new embroidered moccasins, and every woman wore a new tartan shawl. They sang in a strange language songs that had been heard in Europe in the Middle Ages. It was a moving thing to see the silent faces of bronze listening to the wondrous tale. To them the manger was lined with spruce boughs like their own wigwams. They had never seen sheep. They pictured wild deer of the forest peering through the trees. It was a snowshoe trail they saw stretching far to the East whence the Medicine Men came. But it was an authentic Christmas. There was an inner peace and joy on that lonely shore. Next day the children had their hour. A tree stood in the schoolhouse lighted with three inches of wax candle wedged in a hundred rifle cartridges tied to the branches. A bag of candies which shone like rubies, topaz and emeralds waited for every child. A blue goose frozen in its feathers hung high for the oldest grandmother.

The octave ended on New Year's day, the state festival. The ancient Scottish tradition of the old Company was solemnly observed. It was the custom for every Indian to call at the factory and the mission. An anxious bachelor and his dog driver surveyed the ammunition, a bag of flour, a tub of lard, a box of currants, brown sugar and a chest of gunpowder tea. All night long the mud oven was fired. At 10 o'clock the procession started; tea flowed in gallons. The path on the river bank between the church and the old factory was as smooth as the Queen Elizabeth Highway. That night the northern lights came out to serenade the stars.

> *Dear God, they shone in Palestine*
> *Like this, and yon pale moon serene*
> *Looked down among the lowly kine;*
> *On Mary and the Nazarene.*
>
> *The angels called from deep to deep,*
> *The burning heavens felt the thrill,*
> *Startling the flocks of silly sheep*
> *And lonely shepherds on the hill.*

In the morning the tents were down. The mystic visitors were gone. "They departed unto their own home another way."

78

"Then Jesus Came"

THE AFTERGLOW OF CHRISTMAS still shines in the winter sky. The echoes of the angels' song are dying away. It seems like an ironic interlude before the last act of the death struggle of Christian civilization, almost like the awakening of a survivor on a raft in mid-ocean who has been dreaming of his happy home.

The first Christmas I can clearly remember was when I was six years old. We were living in a log cabin on Lake Nipigon—in those days more remote than Aklavik. The Indians lived in birch-bark wigwams in the bitter cold. By December the great trees stood like shrouded commando troops around the clearing, while at night the stars hung, diamond gems, from the rosary of heaven. There were no white children nearer than a hundred miles; no mails in winter.

Suddenly there was an air of mystery. It was hard to bear. Father worked at night with a lantern in the cellar, and mother was always hiding things in a box which was locked. We were told that Jesus was coming, that He came every year in the winter to people who were snowed under.

One morning the five children rushed downstairs from the upper room, where the only heat was from a pipe through the kitchen ceiling. We dressed beside a red-hot stove in the common room. The presents were home-grown—new woollen stockings, beaded moccasins and a pair of snowshoes. There was brown sugar on the porridge and condensed milk which tasted like nectar—it was heaven. But that night I could not sleep because I did not know how I could possibly wait for twelve months. I thought it was a stark-naked miracle, and so it was.

The fact of the Incarnation in a time like this is most significant. Here are four thoughts about Christmas in wartime: Jesus comes as a surprise, and always when He is most needed. The Saviour of the world came in the winter, when the days were short and the nights were long. He was a child of the poor. He chose the lot of the common man. He reversed the standards of society. He passed by the wealth of purple pomp and priestly pride, ignoring Church and State. His throne was the straw in a cattle shed.

Again we notice that it is in the storms of life that Jesus comes. The Sea of Galilee is a microcosm of the world. The disciples were making a night voyage on that turbulent little lake, but when the winds descended from Mount Hermon through the funnel of the Jordan Valley they rowed their hearts out in vain. The storm was too strong. You can drown as easily in Lake Muskoka as in the Atlantic. For the individual a wrecked canoe is as great a tragedy as the Titanic. These men gave up hope. Their Master seemed far away; but He was watching from His altar on the hillside. When all seemed lost, then came Jesus walking on the waves of the sea. Long ago when troops were needed God sent His Son, even as you and me. Christ is not remote from the agony of a million souls. If He is anywhere in the wide world, it is in the ganglion of this cosmic storm. No Christian thinks that the sailors, soldiers and airmen are shut out from Christ when they need Him.

Jesus comes to heal the sick. His angel said: "Thou shalt call His name Jesus, for He shall save His people from their sins." The naked horror of human degeneration is revealed in wartime. It would seem that the moral plague might destroy our race. That statement is not Puritan preaching; it is the simple truth. "All have sinned and come short of the glory of God." There are many stars in the moral sky, but only one Star of Bethlehem.

Jesus came to save men from hopeless sorrow. "Then came Jesus, the doors being shut." The setting of these haunting words is as familiar as the look in the eyes of a friend and as full of nameless peace as the quiet of our own fireside. It was the evening of Easter Day. Jesus was dead. Love was dead. The thoughts of the men within were too bitter and dark for the mocking world without to know and scorn. "Then came Jesus" . . No one heard Him knock. No one unbarred the doors. No one had seen Him enter. Yet there He stood, and with Him came back hope revived, and faith strengthened, and joy alive forever more.

In spite of the impossible, Christ came. He came in spite of their fears, in spite of their doubts, in spite of their own hands barring the doors. "Peace I leave with you, My peace I give unto you: not as the world giveth, give I unto you. Let not your heart be troubled, neither let it be afraid."

79

Bethlehem, Goodnight

THE EYES OF THE WORLD have been turned for the last week upon that little City seven miles south of Jerusalem, on the ridge of Palestine. The lights are going out for another year and, as we say good-bye, let us think of the romantic story of the most famous little City in the world.

All the length of Palestine there is a serrated mountain range from north to south, along which there was a natural highway from time immemorial, looking down three thousand feet westward to the Mediterranean and much more than that eastward to the canyon of the Jordan.

The first time we hear of Bethlehem in history was when Jacob camped at Rama, a mile north, that his beloved wife, Rachel, might be delivered of Benjamin. The beautiful Rachel died there, and that is the reference in the story of the Innocents to Rachel weeping for her children.

Long centuries afterward, Ruth gleaned in the corn fields in the barley harvest and was the heroine of the sweetest idyll of the Old Testament—in fact, the tradition of beautiful women still clings to the place. The story of Mary is in perfect historical harmony and, even today, the women of Bethlehem are the most beautiful in Palestine. There are more Christians here than at Nazareth, and many are the descendants of the Crusaders. Blue eyes and fair hair are not uncommon.

King David, who was the great-grandson of Ruth, was born in Bethlehem. After he became King, when he was fighting one of his fiercest battles, he was besieged by his enemies outside the walls of his native town. He cried out: "O, that some one would bring me drink from the well of Bethlehem." Three of his mighty men cut their way through the Philistine line and brought him the cold water that he had known as a boy. But the hero refused to drink. With a royal gesture he poured it out as a libation to God. From that day to this Bethlehem has been known as the City of David.

The Story of the Nativity is the greatest poem ever written. The shepherds and the wise men are only just disappearing into the January night. But the hopes and fears of all the years have crowned this place with the soft, euphonious name as the Capitol of the World.

The awful war of Vespasian and Titus, which destroyed Jerusalem, made the ancient sites of the land of Jesus a wilderness for two hundred years; but when Constantine became the first Christian Emperor, early in the fourth century, the eyes of the world turned again to the birthplace of Christ. The mother of the Emperor, St. Helena, came to rediscover the cave of the Nativity and to build the great Church, which remains in part the same to the present time. Countless millions have entered the lowly gate into the Babylon-like walls and no one, however skeptical of shrines, can ever resist the sight of the silver star set in the stone with the simple words, in Latin: "Here Jesus Christ was born of the Virgin Mary."

In the fourth and fifth centuries there began a movement which carried thousands of religious folk from

Christian countries to the Holy Land. The canyon of the Jordan was lined with monasteries. The famous Lady Paula came here from Rome to live and die. She was carried on the shoulders of Bishops to her tomb. It was she who wrote: "Hail Bethlehem, House of Bread, wherein was born that Bread that came down from heaven."

Probably the greatest man who ever lived in Bethlehem was St. Jerome, who was the noblest scholar of his age, the man who gave the Bible in Latin, the common tongue of the whole world. When he died the light went out in the western world.

On Christmas Day, 1101 A.D., Baldwin, the Crusader, was crowned the first Christian King of Palestine in the Church of the Nativity.

In the crashing of Empires at the end of the Great War, twenty years ago, the epic of the last Crusade was almost overlooked. It was then that the story was told how the Australians were keeping bivouac on the heights of Bethlehem. Some envious critic replied that he hoped the shepherds watched their flocks.

And so, little City, good-night, till thy star leads the world again next year to the manger.

80

"The Insubstantial Pageant"

MAN IS OF THE EARTH, earthy and a dreamer. He is the most efficient machine ever made. A motor car has no temperament and is foolproof, but it wears out sooner, and man has the unique gift of analyzing himself. It is true that he is so much a part of his material environment that for long periods he forgets that he is an immortal spirit. Suddenly he asks himself: "Where am I going?" What am I doing?" What am I?"

One day a man came in great consternation to Emerson and said: "The world is going to be destroyed; the whole material universe will perish."

"Never mind," said the philosopher; "we shall get on without it."

Religion has always reminded us that we are only transients here. The Prophets often spoke in burning words of "Dies Irae." Poets remind us that "the old earth had a birth long ago, and the old earth must die." The scientists arrive at the same conclusion. They warn us that the solar system is dated, our planet will slow down and freeze to death or some celestial collision will return us to swirling stardust again.

This is bad news for the materialist who has felt no need for spiritual faith. We admit that multitudes of noble men who have sadly given up any idea of personal immortality have found a substitute in their belief in the endless Ascent of Man. They must die in a few short years, but struggle, sacrifice and pain may be worth while if they can bequeath something to the future City of God on Earth.

There is no doubt that for a hundred years before 1914 it was possible for the majority of people born and bred in Europe and America to live their whole lives without serious doubt as to the future of what we called Christian civilization.

Every budding orator of the last generation used to quote Macaulay's word picture of the time when a traveller from New Zealand might stand on the broken arches of London Bridge to sketch the ruins of St. Paul's. It does not seem so fantastic now.

Like Prospero we sometimes feel today that the actors on the world stage are all spirit, and that

The cloud-capped towers, the gorgeous palaces,
The solemn temples, the great globe itself,
Yea, all which it inherit, shall dissolve;
And like this insubstantial pageant faded,
Leave not a rack behind. We are such stuff
As dreams are made on.

We have had enough examples to have made us understand that man's material memories are the poorest of his legacies. The ghostly ruins of Egypt and Babylon are significant only because of the thought of Immortality which their builders showed.

The poor fragments of Hellenic art are useful as examples for modern students. But the philosophy and poetry of their great men have moulded human life ever since.

249

The Coliseum at its finest was not much more impressive than many a football stadium in the modern scene. But Roman law is the possession of all who think.

Leslie Howard, in a broadcast from London on Monday night, points out that in England no one ever considers the material losses caused by bombing. The people have been lifted by suffering to a plane where old standards of daily life seem as but the dust in the balances.

The important things of life seem to be certain qualities which give ultimate satisfaction to human life and which never die:

> *For the things which are seen are temporal.*
> *But the unseen things are eternal.*

81

Sunset

THE ANCIENT BOOK OF ECCLESIASTES is part of the wisdom
literature of the Bible. Some people wonder how it even
got into the sacred volume. The author is popularly regarded as the Omar Khayyam of the Old Testament. A
man disillusioned by life who has seen everything. But
no one can call him dull.

The last chapter of his book is one of the jewel pieces
of the English language. The exquisite poetry of the
lines is so haunting that it almost seems like sacrilege to
explain them. Were it not that many regard the passages
as sheer melody, like the sound of silver bells, it would be
better to leave them alone.

The poem begins with the words "Remember now thy
Creator in the days of thy youth." It tells us why we
should make the morning of life a time for sowing.
"Cast thy bread on the waters: for thou shalt find it after
many days." Don't wait, for a storm is coming. The
imagery of the picture portrays old age as a storm in the
desert. It is an idyll of an Oriental village where after
long sunshine the gathering clouds transform the scene.

First are mentioned the effects of old age on the mental
powers. "Or even the sun, and the light, and the moon,
and the stars be darkened, and the clouds return after
the rain."

The language is highly figurative, but by the sun appears to be meant the intellect or Spirit; the moon will denote the inferior powers of the mind (what the Bible calls the Soul), while the stars may be the five senses which stand halfway between mind and body—that is, the mental powers are enfeebled in old age, the senses no longer responding quickly to stimulus, the memory losing its hold, and certainly the clouds will return after the rain. In childhood and youth, after a rain of tears, the sunshine returns, but it is not so in old age. At this period of life the rain drips on and on, like on a Toronto October day.

In the next verse we have the effects of old age on the body. "In the day when the keepers of the house shall tremble, and the strong men shall bow themselves, and the grinders cease because they are few."

In all languages the body has been compared to a house; but here the different members of the body are not compared to the different parts of the house, but to its different occupants. First the men and then the women. The place of the men is to keep watch. The members employed are the legs and the arms. "The strong men shall bow themselves." These are the keepers, for in old age the limbs shake and shuffle, and the arms grow shrunken and palsied.

Then the women of the house are mentioned. They are called the grinders. No commoner sight meets the observer in any Oriental interior than the women grinding the corn. Another characteristic of Oriental life is the women looking out of the windows. We remember the words of Shakespeare, "Sans teeth, sans everything." Age is certainly characterized by feebleness of vision, especially in the East, where ophthalmia is prevalent.

Thirdly, the effects of old age on the functions of the

252

body are described: "The doors shut in the streets." Impaired hearing: "One shall rise up at the voice of the bird"—experience tells us that it is a common thing as life goes on to have the blessing of sleep denied; it is only the boys and girls who can sleep for ten hours. "The daughters of music shall be brought low"—the music of the voice changes in later years.

Fourthly, the effects of old age on the temper of the mind are described: "They shall be afraid of that which is high." When we are young we can climb mountains; when we are old the breath is scant, and we do not like to undertake the great enterprises that once we should have enjoyed. Old age and "terror shall be in the way." Old age sees all the lions in the path—youth sees not these; it sees only the unattainable. Youth, unaware of its limitations, casts itself without hesitation into enterprises far beyond its power.

"The almond tree shall blossom." The almond tree before it blossoms is one mass of pure white from top to bottom, and so with the white hair that follows the stage of silver threads among the gold. "The grasshopper shall be a burden." The grasshopper is a proverbial image of what is light and trifling, and so mere trifles, the least exertion, is a burden to old age.

"And desire shall fail." The original is the caper berry, which was used by the ancients as a relish to food. And there comes a time in life when all the natural desires and passions gradually atrophy and die.

At this point the poet takes a new start, in order that, having described the frailities of old age, he may characterize death itself, and the phrases in which it is done are incomparable in their beauty:

"Or ever the silver cord be loosed, or the golden bow be

broken, or the pitcher be broken at the fountain, or the wheel be broken at the cistern."

There are two images which come before us here. In the Temple in the midst of the city there is the sacred lamp of solid gold, suspended by silver chains from the ceiling, while the light by which the lamp is kept burning shines in the sanctuary. Night and day the lamp burns steadily on, and to this is compared the flame of vital force continuing to burn in the human organism. But as the storm blows in the door of the Temple the wind rushes under the roof and the silver chain snaps and the bowl is dashed on the marble pavement, and the light goes out. And so in death is the light of life put out.

The other image is equally fine. It is that of an Eastern well, where the water is fetched up from below in a pitcher at the end of a rope, which is wound on a wheel. Thousands of times the pitcher has descended, but some day the pitcher will descend for the last time and the wheel will revolve no more, for it is broken. And how like to this is the action of the lungs and the heart, going on for a lifetime with unfailing regularity, but at last the heart gives its last beat, the lungs expand for the last time, and all is over. Then shall the dust return to God who gave it.

The body of man, fair as it is, is after all but part of the clay of the world, and after its work is done, earth to earth, ashes to ashes, dust to dust. But the spirit of man goes to God, which is its home.

82

The Bivouac of Time

IT IS A MERCIFUL THING that we have come to the end of another year. Sometimes people ask themselves why we have these artificial divisions of time, but, like many another convention which has passed into the stream of our consciousness, apparently without rhyme or reason, there is a profound significance in its influence in our lives.

It is true that time is infinite, without beginning or end, but if anything could drive a man crazy it is to allow himself to brood on the past, thinking through the countless generations of men—back, back through the centuries to the time when monsters waded through the foetid marshes of a half-baked world, even to the period when our planet was a fire ball shot from the gun of some distant sun. And looking into the unknown future is perhaps even more distressing. It is a sound and a safe resolve to revolve within the orbit of what we may understand. We all know that "even the weariest river winds somewhere safe to sea."

First of all, let us look at the romance of the year. A week ago the days began to lengthen. A newborn year is at hand. The light will get stronger and stronger and nature will become more brilliant until the end of June, when everything is in flower, and then that inevitable decline which is part of our human life and seems to belong to all creation will begin.

The autumn, with all its suggestiveness of death, has its influence on every thinking mind. The snow and the winter storms are a fitting requiem for a perfect circle of time, and yet it is not the end. There will still be another year.

We seldom realize that man himself is a parable of the year. He is born a little child with nothing but hope to recommend him. He also passes through the spring, summer, autumn and winter of his existence. Physically, mentally and spiritually he rises to his midsummer, and gradually declines to the sere and yellow leaf. Yet the glory of the Christian religion is that it teaches that when the day of life is done there comes a night and another morning.

Again, the history of the world seems to follow the circumference of the same circle. There is an astonishing similarity in the rise and fall of Empires—Egypt, Babylon, Nineveh, Greece and Rome, to mention only those that are far enough away from us to give us a clear perspective. Each one of these nations had its morning, its noon and its night. Each one made its contribution to the story of mankind, and when even the greatest fell, by some extraordinary Providence there were conserved, for the morning of history, lessons that we could all learn. We know now that the great Empires of the past survived just as long as they had a contribution to make to the destiny of the human race.

Rome ruled the world for half a thousand years. The Hellenic Empire, how short it was!

Thy little day, and yet its grace
From Mountain, Pine and Sea,
The lamp of words lit for the Race
And beauty left for me.

The contribution of the English-speaking people to the story of mankind has been very great, and we like to think that the reason why we have not already become one with Nineveh and Tyre is because, with all our mistakes and failings, there has been a definite Christian character in our civilization.

But behind all these phenomena is the Personality of God. His purpose, His will touches everything that we know and do.

"Lord, Thou hast been our dwelling place in all generations. Before the mountains were brought forth, or ever thou hadst formed the earth and the world, even from everlasting to everlasting, Thou art God. Thou turnest man to destruction; and sayest, Return, ye children of men. For a thousand years in Thy sight are but as yesterday when it is past, and as a watch in the night."

83

Tramp or Pilgrim

WE ARE BEGINNING A NEW MARCH in the history of the world. We are perfectly aware of the fact that philosophers sometimes tell us that there is no division of time, that past, present and future are all one, but the average man at midnight, Dec. 31, stands with reluctant feet as he faces a very real but invisible boundary at the beginning of a new year. The ancient Romans had a god whom they called Terminus; he had two faces, he had no arms or feet, he was a block of marble, but he marked the beginning of things.

As the misty clouds of morning hang over the horizon, we can begin our march of Nineteen Hundred and Forty-five either as a tramp or as a pilgrim. The world is full of people who do not know where they are going, to whom each day brings no challenge and each sunset brings no comfort or work well done. The pilgrim in human life is mankind at his best. From the very beginning of human history the pathfinders of our race have been men with a pilgrim soul. The historic march of the Israelites through the desert is a symbol of the story of humanity, and the first difference between a tramp and a pilgrim is that the pilgrim has a definite end in view. He does not wait to be moved, but he obeys the divine impulse to face the mysterious future with joy and courage, feeling with Browning that "Life is a thing to try the soul's strength upon; who keeps that end in view makes all things serve."

258

The second characteristic of the pilgrim soul is that he believes in the providence of God. Perhaps there has never been a year in modern history when the confidence of decent people in the providence of God has been more sorely tried than in the memorable but unlamented year of 1938. There were so many things that happened which seemed to be contrary to the conventional Christian view of the goodness and the mercy of God. Many times it seemed as if stark brutality was to be the guiding star of modern civilization. The great difficulty is, and has always been, that men expect each succeeding day to see the fulfilment of their ideals in human life. God pays, but He does not pay every night or every week; but the pilgrim mùst be willing to take the long view and to trust that somehow, some time, and somewhere God will justify Himself. There would never have been progress in the development of the soul of mankind if each individual lived a sheltered life in a vaccum secure from all the winds of chance. It is only by moving, only by following the star, that men accomplish a journey which brings them within sight of the City of God.

In the third place, there is no doubt that the spirit of prayer in the individual life is probably the greatest single distinguishing mark between the tramp and the pilgrim soul. There is a sentence in St. Luke's Gospel which gives us a clue: "It came to pass that when Jesus was praying at a certain place His disciples said unto Him, 'Lord, teach us to pray'." It is not for a moment to be supposed that the twelve original Christians never prayed. They had been brought up in religious homes, and probably they had learned to say their prayers as children, even as we. It is evident that these ordinary uninspired men felt the difference between Jesus' prayers and their

259

own: His so strong and sure and real, theirs so weak and stammering; His so God-inspired and prevailing, theirs so erratic and spasmodic. Most of us who call ourselves Christians feel that that is the very weakness in our own lives. We would indignantly deny that we never pray, and yet how much we need to pray as Jesus prayed.

Another difference between the tramp and the pilgrim is that the pilgrim is perfectly certain of God. It is a striking fact that Jesus never argued for the validity of prayer any more than He argued for the existence of God. God was not something to be proved by argument. God was simply there—the beginning and the end of experience. The wellsprings of prayer lie deep down beneath the region of argument. There are certain facts in the life of Christ which serve as an example to everyday men and women distracted by the problems of modern existence, and if we could only grip the truth of these things every one of us might be a pilgrim. Notice that prayer was the habitual atmosphere of the Saviour's daily life. He was never at the mercy of moods, and yet He was no passionless stoic. He knew joy and sorrow, tears and weariness, but through it all His heart turned to prayer like a compass to the north.

And finally, in the pilgrimage of life we learn that prayer is not merely asking for something. The first great pilgrim of the human race, Abraham, the friend of God, talked to his Maker as a man talks to his friend. There can be no friendship in life merely on the basis of benefits received, and the pilgrim who would know the comfort of the divine comradeship will find in communion, thanksgiving, petition and intercession subsistence to our journey's end.

84

The Romance of
the Explorer

EVEN TODAY THE ROMANCE of the north is associated with the legend of the explorer. Probably there never would have been a British North America if it were not for the persistent dream of the Northwest Passage through Hudson's Bay to Cipango and Cathay.

It is a strange thing that the early explorers of Canada for the most part were not Canadians. It was the new-comer who dared. Alexander Mackenzie was the kind of man whose story sounds like fiction. He was born on the Island of Lewis in the outer Hebrides in the year 1763, just after the fall of the French Empire in Canada. Within twenty years Scottish business men in Montreal had combined with French Canadian voyageurs to found the famous Northwest Company. It was the first and so far the last perfect example of the blending of the French and British spirit on Canadian soil.

They at once challenged the commercial supremacy of the staid and conservative Hudson's Bay Company. The spirit of these adventurers was seen in the Beaver Club in Montreal where after dinner the members, whose gold medals showed that they had wintered in the North, sat on the floor as if they were paddling a birch-bark canoe. With fire tongs or swords for paddles they swung to the music of a mystic canoe.

Young Alexander Mackenzie arrived, a boy of twenty, to join these argonauts. After a four year's apprenticeship, during which he must have revealed great gifts, he was chosen as a partner to command Fort Chippeweyan. For a young man of twenty-four it was a great opportunity to succeed Peter Pond on Lake Athabasca—the Gateway of the Arctic.

There were three elements which converged to light a beacon in Canadian history, the man, the place and the time. First, the right time had come. Pioneers had struggled, lived and died for two hundred years without solving the mystery of the Northwest. The fur traders had mapped the interior but no man had yet found Canada's Northern or Western Ocean. For all they knew it might extend to the Pole.

Secondly, Athabasca Lake was the Mediterranean of the Northwest—the meeting place of waters from the western mountains and the Slave, which Indians said was a bypath to a frozen hell.

In the third place the man had arrived. This young Scotsman was a born explorer. He had a vision, boundless energy and ruthless determination.

On June 3rd, 1789, Mackenzie left Fort Chippeweyan with three canoes, four French Canadians and a young German named Steinbeck. In a day they reached the Slave River. Rousing his men every morning at five o'clock, they sped down stream at the rate of sixty-seven miles a day. On June 9th they reached Great Slave Lake, where they had to drag their canoes through the ice floes. They were warned that they would take years to reach the sea. The Indians told of monsters and banks of fire. On July 5th they passed Great Bear River. They began to see the midnight sun on July 14th, 1789, the very day of the storming of the Bastile. The tide invaded their tents. Icebergs and whales told them that they had reached their goal. Returning against the swift stream they tracked for hundreds of miles along the shore. On September 12th, 1789, he was back at Chippeweyan. He was absent one hundred and two days and had travelled three thousand miles. He called his river the Disappointment. He was not interested in icebergs and his Company thought his journey of no importance.

The character of Mackenzie is revealed by the fact that he went at once to London to procure scientific instrument to study astronomy and engineering.

In September, 1792, he left Chippeweyan again. He built a fort and wintered at Peace River Crossing. On May 17th, 1793, he plunged again into the gorge of the Peace River, climbing through the rapids into the most beautiful park land in North America. Vast herds of elk and buffalo surrounded them. On May 24th they portaged over the Divide with the white mountain peaks laughing at them. On May 31st they were at the forks of the Finlay. Through the Bad River and the Parsnip they floated to the Fraser on June 23rd. They made the vital decision to leave their canoe and make an overland journey. They met tribes of salmon eating Indians who camped in lofty houses, built ten feet above the ground. He crossed the entrance to Bentinck Arm to Bella Coola where he inscribed on the rocks with vermillion— "Alexander Mackenzie from Canada, by land, the 22nd of July, one thousand, seven hundred and ninety-three." A perfect hunter of fame. Two chances at immortality; he takes them, one with each barrel.

The partners of the Northwest Company were only mildly interested. There was an eagle in the barnyard.

The young pathfinder refused to be tamed. He was too big for his future. In a short time he returned to England where he became a vital factor in the big business of the fur trade. It was he who first suggested union with the Hudson's Bay Company. But it all seems an anticlimax. He ceased to live when his canoe had no more rapids to run.

85

The Tragedy of
the Explorer

MEN NEED POETS TO SET THEIR LIVES to music. Today it is
the fashion to sneer at the Victorians. Their age seems
too safe and they certainly were sure that they were
bound for the millennium. Browning deduces the infinite
good nature of God from the pages of a furniture cata-
logue, while the "poisonous honey" of Swinburne only
appealed to those who wore red ties and long hair. We
may have laughed at the man in Tennyson who—

> *"Walked between his wife and child,*
> *And now and then he gravely smiled."*

O, if we could only do it now!

The nineteenth century was saved from utter materialism by its adventurers. It was the great age of explora-
tion. In nothing is the British character more truly
revealed than in this fascinating field.

Sir John Franklin, like Captain Robert Scott of the
Antarctic, was a naval officer. Both died tragic deaths.
Both were failures from the point of view of smooth
efficiency. Both blundered and slogged their way to immortality. Above all, both are loved by their country, not
for what they did so much as for what they were.

John Franklin as a young lieutenant made his first
Polar expedition the year after Waterloo. The "Dorothea"

and "Trent" reached 80°34 North of Spitzbergen, but were obliged to return. Franklin's courage made him a marked man.

In 1819 Captain Franklin was chosen to lead an expedition from Hudson's Bay into the Mackenzie Basin towards the Arctic Sea. Making his headquarters at Fort Chippeweyan, he plunged into the North. He spent two years between Great Slave Lake and the mouth of the Coppermine River. The story of their hardships and disasters is almost too harrowing to the reader. The journals of Franklin, Dr. Richardson and Back tell of man's heroism which endures when every hope was gone. During the second summer they descended the Coppermine to Bloody Falls where Samuel Hearne had witnessed the massacre of the Eskimos in July, 1771. Then their Indians left them. The half-breed interpreters tried to escape, sensing the coming winter, while the white men entered the months of snow and darkness loaded down with heavy, useless equipment. Growing weaker they abandoned all but their journals as they crept half frozen across the barren lands. They did not know how to kill the cariboo. The chief food was tripe de roche or reindeer moss, and roasted deerskins or shoes from camps. As some became too weak to move, Franklin pushed on to get relief. At the last extremity he staggered into the post at Fort Providence with the cry, "Merciful God, we are saved."

The relief party saved most of the main camp, but a crazed Iroquois Guide who was discovered with meat that came from a frozen comrade suddenly shot Hood as he was reading Bickersteth's Scripture Help. Dr. Richardson shot him through the head with a pistol to save the others. After the survivors were reunited, the leader

266

made this entry in his journal. "I went a few yards from the house today in search of bones and returned quite fatigued, having found but three."

"The doctor again made incisions in Adam's legs, which discharged a considerable quantity of water and gave him great relief. We read prayers and a portion of the New Testament in the morning and evening, as has been our practice, and I may remark that the performance of these duties always afforded us the greatest consolation, serving to strengthen our hope in the mercy of the Omnipotent who alone could save and deliver us." There speaks the authentic voice of the Victorian age. They travelled in the Arctic five thousand, five hundred and fifty miles.

The third journey lasted two years and covered much of the same territory, but came into the lower reaches of the Mackenzie for the first time.

In July, 1825, Franklin arrived in America with his old friends Richardson and Back. They had learned much and had hopes which were partly fulfilled. After descending to the mouth of the Mackenzie the party divided. Richardson turned west along the coast towards Alaska. He gave his name to the glorious Richardson Range which every midnight in June turns from blue to scarlet and then to amber when viewed from Aklavik.

Franklin emerged through the Eastern Channel. He was met by hundreds of primitive Eskimos who stormed his whale boats with shameless curiosity and good humour. A great party of his store of trading goods was stolen. At one time it seemed as if a gun shot from his crew might have meant the finish of his expedition. He reached his headquarters at Coronation Gulf. He never reached the great Arctic Islands. He explored Great Bear

Lake. The Expedition ended in 1827, having charted one thousand miles of the Arctic coast line. Enough had been done for honour. He had earned a rest.

After an interval of eighteen years he came back. The mystery of the Northwest Passage was unsolved. A contemporary portrait reveals Sir John Franklin as a rotund middle aged man. He looks like the Prince Consort. But the old fire still burned.

On May 26th, 1845, he sailed in command of two fine vessels, "Erebus" and "Terror" to find the Northwest Passage. He wrote from Baffin Bay two months later. The rest was silence.

For ten years the whole world sought him in vain. The Admiralty offered a reward of ten thousand pounds for authentic news. Dr. John Rae of the Hudson's Bay Company, a genius of Arctic travel, who lived on his journeys like an Eskimo, and solved the problem of living off the country half a century before Nansen, wrote to the Admiralty in July, 1855, that he had learned from the Eskimos that four years before forty white men had been met dragging a whale boat across the frozen sea to the shores of King William Land. Their bodies had been found later and from the contents of the kettles it was evident that they had been driven to the last resource of cannibalism. The complete story was known when Captain McClintock of the yacht "Fox" returned in 1858. This final expedition was sent out by Lady Franklin. Sir John Franklin died on June 11th, 1847. The ships were abandoned on April 22nd, 1848. The men dropped in their tracks like milestones to the coast. A pathetic treasure of relics on the most northerly island of Canada speaks forever of the tragedy of the explorer.

86

Man, the Enemy

WE HAVE COME TO THINK that the human race is the only thing that dignifies this very minor planet. If a man ever feels unduly important, northing will cure him more quickly than a visit to the Arctic. The farther he goes, the smaller he will seem to himself. After all, two-thirds of the surface of the globe is salt water, and there is room there to bury the pet of creation and all his works.— The first sense of conquest, as the aeroplane speeds north, soon fades. The mountains are not impressed. The rocks are not kind to him; the river has no mind to him. He is only the shadow of a cloud. We are not the only living things. Other lesser forms of life were here before us. If they could all vote, it is quite probable that homo sapiens would be declared public enemy number one. His attitude towards them is very like the Japanese benevolent Mission to China.

In the Book of Common Prayer, there is a remarkable canticle used as an alternative for the Te Deum. The Benedicite goes back to natural religion "O All ye Works of the Lord, Bless ye the Lord, Praise Him and Magnify Him for ever." The fishes, beasts and birds are given their place with man among created beings. Even the trees seem to be endowed with personality. Francis of Assisi's Canticle of the Sun, in which he calls the elements his sisters and brothers, shows that one can be a Christian and a lover of nature too. It seems reasonable to admit that emotion is shared. If the living things of creation have an effect upon us, perhaps we also stir something in their elemental lives.

The poor fish have little cause to love us. The most exclusive lordly speckled trout in the world used to live in the Nipigon River—a clear, flashing stream which runs for thirty miles over rocks between two of the coldest, purest lakes in North America. Salmo Fontinalis was King—no lesser could breed there. Man came, with his eye on the main chance, and built a saw mill to pollute the sanctuary with bark and saw-dust. Someone else got a concession to build a dam at each end of the river. The few aristocrats still remaining at Virgin Falls probably have the same opinion of the human race as Timon of Athens.

The blue waveys are the rarest and shyest of birds. They breed in Baffins Land and winter in Southern California. James Bay is the half-way resting place, where the vast flocks alight to give the young a chance to grow and fatten for the final migration to the Pacific swamps. What bed-time stories must be told in the nests of Pangnatung! About the murderous guns; the Indian means death. It is not flattering to us to witness the look of petrified horror in the eyes of a young deer who has winded. The alien scent of Gulliver's Yahoo.

Forests have always been enchanted. It is not only the love of scenery which stirs the heart, but the feeling of a presence. Everything which rises from a seed of life, which grows after an unvaried form, with leaves of a strict pattern, probably has a dim consciousness of its own. George Macdonald wrote a famous book—Phantastes—

which speaks of the Spirit of the Forest. He says that all trees are, according to their nature, hostile or friendly. We think it more likely that they are a great family who stick together. It is their only protection against the stranger, for they cannot move and they are dumb. The old legends of the Faun, the Satyr, and the Spirits of the Wild may not be mere imagination but may signify a clash of elements. The sense of being lost in the woods, which is one of the most terrible of human experiences, is far more than missing a path. It can rise to the plane of sheer, mystic terror of unseen adversaries. The underbrush which sticks its hands in the face of an intruder, is a warning to keep out. Vegetable things must often resent the wild vandalism of creatures who rush from motor cars on the twenty-fourth of May to drag blossom-laden branches bleeding from a living trunk. For all we know, a grove of pines may be looking with frozen horror on the log house built of their relations. The light shining through the window, the ghostly suggestion of a candle in a pumpkin on Hallowe'en.

Fires to a forest are what wars are to humanity, the greatest of all disasters. The forest meets disaster with all the dignity of mankind at its best. First, there is the black interval of mourning. When the flames and smoke are over, all seems ruin. Then nature goes to work— from other areas, seeds are blown. Here and there, the blessed rain starts new growth from the roots; flowers bloom with Jazz-like abandon. The cardinal purple of the fireweed covers the ruin. In a few years, there is a new forest or a new civilization; but here and there may be seen black stumps standing uncompromising in the verdure as a sign of remembrance.

87

Invasion

THE ANCIENT BOOK OF DANIEL presents a series of pictures like titanic frescoes from some Eastern temple. In the famous fifth chapter a deadly warning flashes on the walls of a banquet house. The lightning discloses the target. The thunder follows as the bomb of ruin falls.

The old Bible writers were great artists. Here is a true night-piece with all the colors of the extravagant riot of luxury and passion, the growing madness and bewilderment of a stricken dance hall or a torpedoed liner on the Irish coast. It is as modern as radio.

In the words of Farrar, "Night was about to come down upon Babylon. The shadows of her two hundred and fifty towers began to lengthen. The Euphrates rolled on, touched by the fiery splendor of the setting sun. The gates of brass opened and shut like doors of flame. The hanging gardens, wet with heavy dew, began to pour from starlit flowers a fragrance for many miles around. The weird colossal cherubim on the temple of Bel kept the watch of death over the capital of the known world."

Hitler is giving a Victory Ball. Beauty and chivalry conspire to make him shine. A mortal man sits upon a jeweled throne which—

> *Outshines the wealth of Ormuz or of Ind*
> *Or where the gorgeous East with richest hand*
> *Showers on its kings barbaric pearl and gold.*

272

As the supper goes on the madness increases. They pledge their gods of brass and stone in the sacred cups which had once stood in the Temple of the Eternal.

But what is that upon the plaster? Like a modern electric sign, high on the wall, there glows a message from heaven which seems to throb. "Is it a phantom? Is it a god?" The goblets fall. There is a cry of horror. A plain, forgotten prophet is hurried in to read the doom.

"Mene, mene, tekel, upharisin."

There was short space for repentance. The Mede was at the gate. That night the waters of the Euphrates were dammed up by a besieging army. Under the gates in solid phalanx the avengers marched in. There is a tramp of soldiers on the steps; there is a clash of axes on the doors. There are shrieks, spilled wine, the blood of women, and the carcass of what was once a king.

> *That night they slew him on his father's throne;*
> *He died unnoticed and the hand unknown,*
> *Crownless and sceptreless Belshazzar lay,*
> *A robe of purple round a form of clay.*

The message of God, which is for every age and for every race of men, and for every man and woman who ever lived, is mysterious, as all His words are. The four words are four weights. A mina, a mina, a shekel, and a half-mina. The original meaning was numbered, weighed and divided. The first word is repeated to remind us that we have many warnings. Belshazzar had known the history of his own father. Daniel in his solemn condemnation says to the king: "Thou knewest all this . . . the God in whose hand thy breath is, and whose are all thy ways, hast thou not glorified." God had numbered the sins of Babylon till they overflowed. Again the opportunities of the king were numbered. No man in ancient history had a greater opportunity. With his wild and gifted father as an example, his end might have been different. The wages of sin is death. They are not paid every week, but they are paid.

The second is "weighed"—"Thou art weighed in the balances, and art found wanting." The patience of God is wonderful, and yet we cannot read the story of nations without observing that God has weighed every empire in the long story of man. We see them all through the centuries. Their struggles, their glories, their rise and fall. Greece and Rome, Spain and Britain. The pattern becomes clearer through the distance. Some are gone, and as for ourselves—we still live. The voice of God still calls. There is no enemy from without which can destroy us unless in the scales of Eternal Justice we shall be found wanting. Then and then only we shall pass into the twilight and see our pomp of yesterday is one with Nineveh and Tyre. It need not be a long and painless process. It is a startling thing to reflect how quickly great empires have passed when the right time comes.

God weighs Churches. Christianity has had a long innings. We believe that Christ is God's last Word to men. He has promised to be with His Church to the end of the world. But no weight of historic grandeur, no glory of ritual will save any Church in this modern world. God is weighing the bishops and clergy, the choir and the building—all go into the scales. The only object of the visible Christian Church is to save the souls of men.

The last word is "divided." Here we come to the thought which we all seek to avoid: the fact that God observes individuals. The widest significance of conscience is that there comes a time when a man cannot hide in a crowd. God will divide the good from the evil in human life. There comes a Day when each must stand before the Great White Throne, when the Book of Remembrance will be opened, when we shall be revealed to the world and to ourselves as we really are.

We are living our careless lives conscious that we are 5,000 miles from the Dance of Death in Europe. But death is an old sportsman, and takes his quarry on the wing.